The Science of Bharata Natyam

The Science of Bharata Natyam

SAROJA VAIDYANATHAN
(Padma Bhushan Awardee)

KANISHKA PUBLISHERS, DISTRIBUTORS
NEW DELHI-110 002

KANISHKA PUBLISHERS, DISTRIBUTORS
4697/5-21A, Ansari Road, Daryaganj
New Delhi -110 002
Phones : 2327 0497, 2328 8285
Fax : 011-2328 8285
E-mail : kanishka_publishing@yahoo.co.in
kanishkabooks@gmail.com

First Published-1984
Second Edition-2000
Edition-2026

ISBN: 978-81-7391-388-9

PHOTOGRAPHY: NANDLAL
ILLUSTRATIONS: RAGHUVIR SINGH AKELA
SECRETARIAL ASSISTANCE: B.R. BALAJI
SKETCHES BY C.V. KAMESH AND HIMANSHU
PROOF READING BY HIMANSHU SRIVASTAVA

PRINTED IN INDIA

Published by Madan Sachdeva for Kanishka Publishers, Distributors, 4697/5-21A, Ansari Road, Daryaganj, New Delhi-110002, Typeset by Sunshine Graphics, Delhi, and Printed at G.S. Printers, Delhi.

पूजादिष्वनुराग।

"In the worship of the Lord with deep love and firm attachment"

Foreword

Bharata Natyam as an art form has seemed to me to embody the whole gamut of Indian expression in all its richness, its variety, and its nuances. The fact that it has emerged through two thousand years of history with its purity and transcendental quality is tribute to its inherent vitality.

Over the last few decades it has attracted many a dedicated practitioner who has preserved its essence and enriched its content. Saroja Vaidyanathan is one such votary. Her untiring zeal in propagating the art and science of Bharata Natyam is renowned. In this book, aptly titled 'The Science of Bharata Natyam', Smt. Vaidyanathan explains in lucid language and clear cut line drawings the technical elements that go to make this magnificent dance form.

Bharata Natyam is a dance that commands the intricacies of a science and infuses these with the imagination and depth of an art. The book, I am sure, will be equally useful to the layman and intiate at home and abroad.

P.V. Narasimha Rao

आङ्गिकं भुवनं यस्य वाचिकं सर्ववाङ्मयम् ।
आहार्यं चन्द्रतारादि तं नुमः सात्विकं शिवम् ।।

We bow to the eternal Shiva the God for dance who has the whole world as his garment, whose language is universal and whose attributes are the moon, the stars etc.

Preface

The present book is an outcome of several years of research into the theory and practice of Bharatanatyam. Being the third generation of guru-shishya *parampara* of Tanjavur, Kattumannar Muthukumaran Pillai and a direct disciple of Guru K. Lalitha, I have received rigorous training in Bharatanatyam. I have also been trained in Karnatic Music under Prof. P. Sambamurthi at the University of Madras. With the experience of fifty five years as a performing artiste, Guru, and the Founder of Ganesa Natyalaya, a leading institute of classical dance, I could perceive the vista of the origin and the progress of Bharatanatyam in all its splendour and glory. The art may be compared to the ocean or to cosmos; the deeper one goes into it, the more there is to comprehend and appreciate. Similarly there is no limit to the scope for innovation within the grammar of Bharatanatyam.

During my recitals, lecture-demonstrations, and classes, I discovered a deep desire for a comprehensive understanding of this art amongst both connoisseurs and students, regardless of their individual cultures. In this book, therefore, I have attempted to provide an insight into the several aspects of Bharatanatyam, complete with illustrations and diagrams, to assist the reader on the long and exciting journey of appreciation of the art.

I owe my gratitude to my Gurus, my parents and my family, without whose support and assistance, it would not have been possible for me to accomplish this task.

Saroja

श्री वेंकटाचलपतये नमः

तस्मिन्ननन्यता तद्विरोधिषूदासीनता च।

Whole-hearted and single minded devotion and detachment to all else with complete indifference is Renunciation

Narada-Bhakti Sutra

Bharatanatyam

Classical Dance	:	Bharatanatyam
State of Origin	:	Tamil Nadu
Earlier Names	:	Devadasi Attam, Sadir Attam, Chinna Melam and Koothu
Basic Posture	:	Araimandi (half bending posture), Muzhumandi (sitting on the toes with knees apart), Samapadam (standing posture with feet together)
Style of Music	:	Carnatic Music
Instruments	:	Mridangam, Talam, Ghatam, Kanjeera, Violin, Veena, Tambura, Flute, Nadaswaram, Harmonium, Morsingh
Fundamental Movements	:	Adavu, Hasta
Repertoire	:	Pushpanjali, Alarippu, Jathiswaram, Shabdam, Varnam, Padam, Javali, Keertanam, Ashtapadi, Bhajan, Viruttam, Namavali, Thillana and Mangalam
Languages	:	Sanskrit, Tamil, Telugu, Kannada, Malayalam, Hindi and Marathi
Composers	:	Ponnayya, Chinnayya, Sivanandam, Vadivelu, Papanasam Sivan, Purandara Dasa, Poochi Srinivasa Iyengar, Subarayar Iyer, Dandayuthapani Pillai, Oothukadu Venkata Subbaiyar, Subramaniam Bharathi, Swathi Thirunal, Jayadeva and many other Bhakthi poets and saints
Styles	:	Tanjavur, Pandanallur, Vazhuvur, Kalakshetra
Shastras (Texts)	:	Natya Shastra and Abhinaya Darpanam
Debut Performance	:	Arangetram
Symbol on Stage	:	Nataraja

Contents

CHAPTER-1

INTRODUCTION

Culture is a portmanteau expression indicating a fusion of several aspects that condition and are in turn conditioned by the life and civilisation of the people. Culture is what distinguishes the different peoples of the world. It includes religion, language, attire, attitudes, painting, music, dance, other performing arts and a host of other things. As an essential aspect or ingredient, dance helps identify the culture, taste and attitude of the people. In a large multi-lingual country like India, culture would not represent a single unified set of values or ideas but would indeed be multi-dimensional in character depending on the cross fertilization of ideas, values and systems obtaining in the different parts of the country. That is why, it is said that India and Indian culture are examples par excellence of unity in diversity. It would not be an exaggeration to say that *Bharata Natyam* occupies a prominent position in the Indian cultural profile. One has to go to the remote past to trace the origin of this form of fine art which is inextricably associated with religion and mythology. *Bharata Natyam* emanated in the southern part of India;

the temple carvings and sculptures bear ample testimony to this assertion. Temples, apart from being places of worship, provided in the ancient days the forum for socio-cultural interaction of the people. With their vast courtyards and halls, the temples became the natural venue in the southern part of India where cultural programmes used to be held, the illumination being provided by huge oil lamps. For reasons not clearly known, dance became the exclusive preserve of *devadasis.* The expression *devadasi* literally means God's attendant or devotee. *Devadasis,* therefore, came to be attached to particular temples and it was their duty to give recitals in praise of the presiding deity of the temple. This would partly explain the religious and mythological base of *Bharata Natyam.* For a long time, it was commonly known as *Sadir* or *Sadir-āttam* in Tamil and was patronised by *Maharajahs* and *Zamindars.* It is not necessary to dwell on the vicissitudes through which *Bharata Natyam* went. Suffice it to say that thanks to the sustained efforts of enlightened art lovers and social workers, this fine art was restored to its pristine glory and status and it regained the respectability that it has been enjoying since the last forty years or so. Youngsters of respectable families evinced considerable interest and started learning *Bharata Natyam* and there is hardly any part of India at present where *Bharata Natyam* as a dance form is not known, taught or performed; it is popular even internationally.

If exactness is the hallmark of science, *Bharata Natyam* may indeed be described as a science amongst the performing arts. It is exact in the sense that it places equal emphasis on the different aspects that go to make a dance, namely, *Bhava* (expression), *Raga* (melody) and *Tala* (rhythm). *Natyam* in Tamil means dance and the prefix *Bharata* is commonly explained as an acronym composed of the first letters of *Bhava, Raga,* and *Tala.* There is also a theory that *Bharata Muni* laid down the first principles of this form of dance and hence it is called *Bharata Natyam.*

नटनभेदाः

एतच्चतुर्विधोपेतं नटनं त्रिविधं स्मृतम्

नाट्यं नृत्तं नृत्यमिति मुनिभिर्भरतादिभिः।

According to Bharata Muni and others, Nritta, Nritya and Natya are the three aspects of dance.

Performing arts were classified as *nritta, nritya* and *natya* in our ancient classics. *Nritta* refers to the pure form of dance comprising foot-work and the movements of limbs, neck, head etc. The *nritta* conforms to the rhythm or beat or tala and is intended to be a delineation of graceful and artistic movements. It does not, however, seek to convey any meaning. The *nritta* is, therefore, performed either to the utterance of the *jati, korvai, teermanams* etc. or to the singing of simple notes or *swara* combinations which are repeated a number of times. *Alarippu, jatiswaram* and *tillana* fall under this category.

Nritya places the emphasis on *abhinaya* (facial expression) and gestures to convey certain meaning or message. The combination of *abhinaya* and *nritta* is called *nritya. Sabdam, varnam* and *padam* may be classified as *nritya.*

Natya denotes the drama form a performing art comprising *abhinaya,* gestures and dialogue or spoken words which could be easily followed by the audience. In a sense, Lord *Shiva's tandava* dance may be taken to be the first form of *nritta* and *Parvati's lasya,* the origin of *nritya.*

नाट्योत्पत्ति
ऋग्यजुः सामवेदेभ्यो वेदाच्चाथर्वणः क्रमात्
पाठ्यं चाभिनयं गीतं रसान् संगृह्य पद्मजः

नाट्यवेदं ददौ पूर्वं भरताय चतुर्मुखः।
ततश्च भरतः सार्धं गन्धर्वाप्सरसां गणैः।।
नाट्यः नृत्तं तथा नृत्यमग्रे शम्भोः प्रयुक्तवान्।
प्रयोगमुद्धतं स्मृत्वाः स्वप्रयुक्तं ततो हरः।।
तण्डुना स्वगणाग्रण्या भरताय न्यदीदिशत्।
लास्यमस्याग्रतः प्रीत्वा पार्वत्या समदीदिशत्।।

Puranas have it that Lord *Shiva* danced sixteen varieties of cosmic dance including the *Ananda Tandava.* From His small *damaroo* (drum), *kinkini* and other attributes, flowed the grammar and nuances of the dance which Lord *Brahma* imbibed. And, Lord *Brahma* took the compositions of *Rig Veda,* the expressions of *Yajur Veda,* the music of *Sama Veda* and the *rasa of Atharva Veda* and synthesised them with the dance to form the *Shastra. Nandikeshwara* was inspired by the *Shastra* and passed it on to *Bharata Muni.* When he codified this dance form and presented it before Lord *Shiva,* He felt that this form of dance could best be rendered by females, whereupon His consort *Parvati* pleased Lord *Shiva* by performing the dance. It is also interpreted that whereas Lord *Shiva gave the nritta,* it was *Parvati* who embellished it with *lasya* and the two namely *nritta* and *lasya* were constituted by *Bharata Muni* into a dance form and hence it is called *Bharata Natyam.* The point that it synthesises the best elements of the four *vedas* raises it to the position of the fifth *veda.*

Science and technology which have made life easy in practically every respect have benefitted the performing arts too. The oil lamps, romantic as they were, have given way to electric lights. The singer does not have to strain her vocal cords as much as one had to in the olden days. The microphone and the loudspeakers carry the voice of the singer to the farthest corners of the assembly. The dancer does not have to dance on the stone floor any longer; the stages are now provided with smooth wooden floor. With the provision of such modern facilities, it has become possible for the artiste to make innovations without exceeding the limits of the grammar of *Bharata Natyam.*

The introduction of ballet or dance-drama is one such innovative effort. The ballet, being a beautiful synthesis of the elements of *Nritya* and *Natya,* has been adopted as a convenient and colourful form of presenting epics in the dance form. A solo dancer has a certain freedom of execution of the dance while a ballet calls for a high degree of synchronisation of movements without letting them appear mechanical. Choreographing a ballet requires a lot more of attention to details and demands greater skills and perception. Even the selection of artistes to portray the different characters in a ballet has to be done with plenty of care.

Bharata Natyam as an art had been highly developed even 2000 years ago. Its theory and practice had been systematised and codified in elaborate treatises like *Bharata's Natya Shastra* and *Nandikeswara's Abhinaya Darpana.* Yet it is not something antiquated; it is fresh and fascinating now as it was in ancient times. Neither old nor new, it is an art for eternity because of the outstanding renaissance work of tar-seeing pioneers and also because of the enduring and enthralling beauty of the art itself.

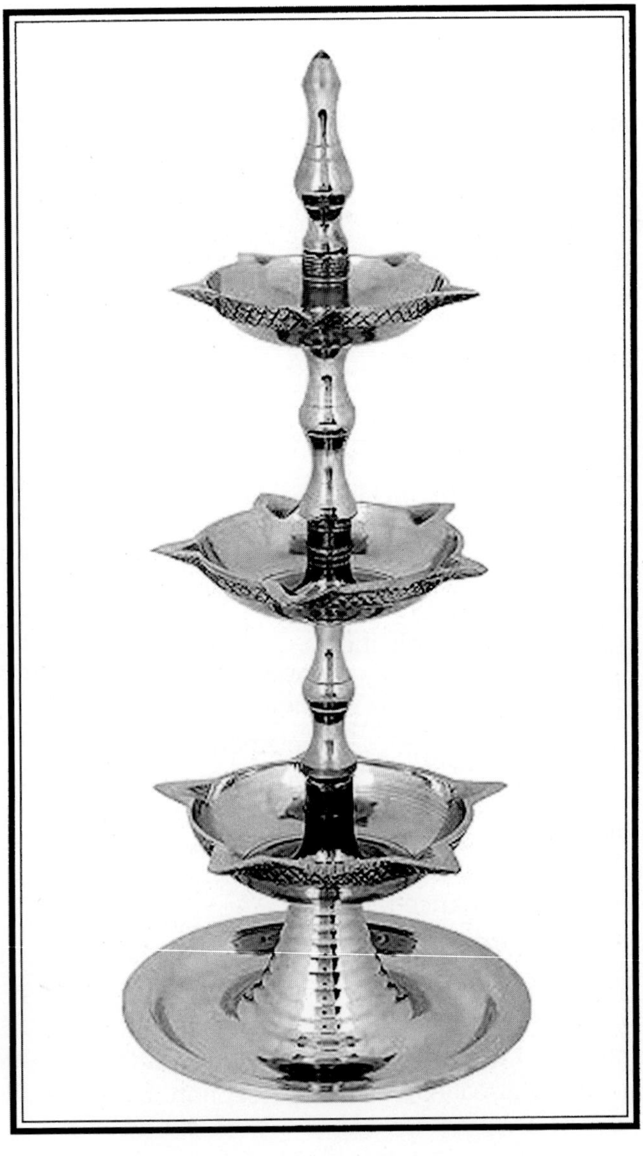

CHAPTER-2

ADAVU
(Foot Work)

नृत्तम्
भावभिनयहीनं तु नृत्तमित्यभिधीयते ।।

Nritta *is devoid of any expression or emotion.*

Elsewhere in this book, the delineation of the 35 talas with 175 ramifications has been referred to and it has been pointed out that every composer chooses an appropriate tala to suit the metre and rhythm of the composition. In a dance, the footwork and the hand movements are so organised as to conform to the *tala*. In doing so, a variety of permutations and combinations of the beats are formed. The basic element of such formations is the *adavu*. A number of *adavus* put together form the first chain called the *korvai*. A group of *korvais* alongwith the *Sollukattu* of a *guru* or *nattuvanar* is collectively referred to as *jati*, and an intricate sequence of *jatis* gives the *teermanam*. To facilitate understanding, an *adavu* can be likened to a streamlet, a *korvai* to a stream, a *jati* to a tributary to a river and the *teermanam* to a big river, majestic and fascinating.

The *adavus* that are in vogue are described below:

(*i*) *Tattadavu:* standing in *ardha mandala* pose and striking the foot flat on the floor.

(*ii*) *Nāttu Adavu:*

(*a*) Standing in *ardha mandala* pose and stretching one leg forward with heel on the floor and toes up.

(*b*) Standing in *ardha mandala* pose and placing one leg with the toes on the floor and heel up.

(*iii*) *Kudittu Adavu:* Standing in *ardha mandala* pose, jumping a little and landing on the toes and thereafter bringing the heels down with force.

(*iv*) *Tattimettu:* Standing in *ardha mandala* pose, one foot (usually the left foot) is placed straight and the other foot is placed side-ways, the heel of the right foot being near the middle of the left foot.

The time units of 3, 4, 5, 7 and 9 are generally used in *tattimettu adavu.* They are called *Tisra (3), Chaturasra (4), Khanda (5), Misra (7)* and *Sankeerna (9)* and the technical words for these are—

1. Ta-ki-ta (3)
2. Ta-ka-dhi-mi (4)
3. Ta-ka-ta-ki-ta (5)
4. Ta-ka-dhi-mi-ta-ki-ta (7)
5. Ta-ka-dhi-mi-ta-ka-ta-ki-ta (9)

(*v*) *Sarukkal:* Sitting in *mandi* position, raise the torso slighly and slide one foot sidewards with toes down and heel up. The face and the torso are turned to the other side.

Some of the *hastas* are used for *Adavu's;* they are called *Nritta hastas.* They are *Shikara, Patāka, Alapadma, Tripatāka, Dolā, Kapittha, Katakāmukha, Chatura, etc.* These *hastas* when they are combined with *adavus* have no meaning. They are just ornamental displays.

Hastas or hand gestures are explained in the next chapter. However, it would be useful to mention here that generally *kapittha, dola, ardhapatāka* and *shikara hastas* are used in *tattimettu adavu,* and *tripatāka, alapadma* and *katakāmukha* are prominent in *kudittu adavu,* whereas in *sarukkal, shikara hasta* and *patāka hasta* are used. Most of the *nritta hastas* are used in *nattu adavu.*

The utterance of the expressions depicting the *jati* and *teermanam* by the *guru* or *nattuvanār* (Conductor) is called *Sollukattu* and the dancer gets the cue for the various steps, footwork and movements from the *Sollukattu.*

The fine distinction between the *korvai* on the one hand and the *jati* and the *teermanam* on the other hand is that even without the utterance of the *Sollukattu* and merely going by the sounds produced by the cymbals and the percussion instrument, the dancer can dance to the *korvai*, but the *jati* and the *teermanam* can be executed only with the *guru* or *nattuvanār* uttering the *Sollukatu*. The *teermanams* are dominantly seen in *varnam* in which these are intricately woven, based on three *layas* and five *gatis*. The *korvai* and *jati* occur in all *nritta* items like *alarippu*, *jatiswaram*, *varnam* and *tillana* as well as in selected *padams* like those portraying Lord *Shiva*'s cosmic dance.

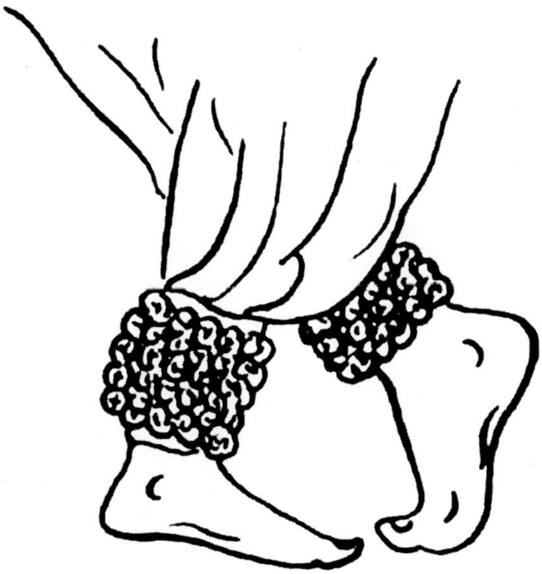

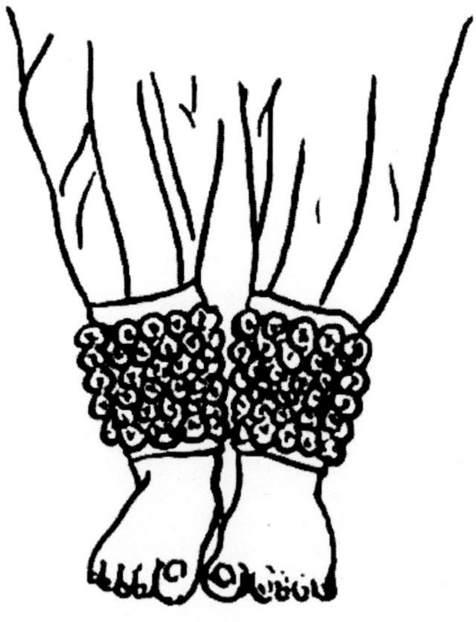

STANDING POSE

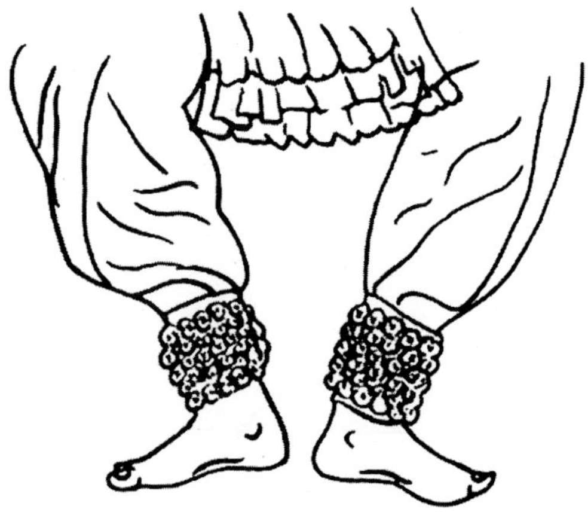

TATTADAVU

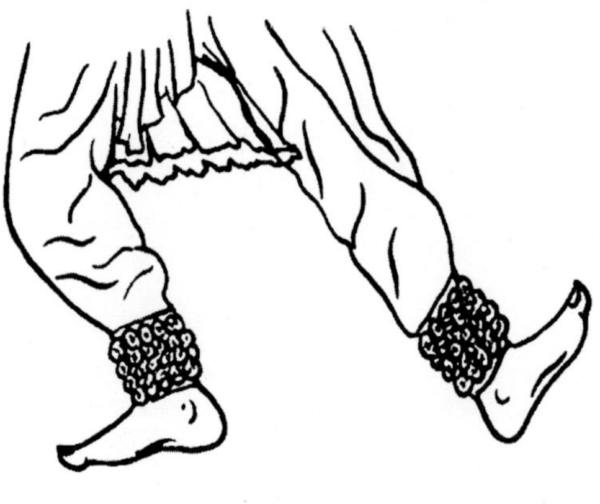

NĀTTU ADAVU

TATT1-METTU

SARUKKAL ADAVU

MANDI

ARAI MANDI (ARDHA MANDALA)

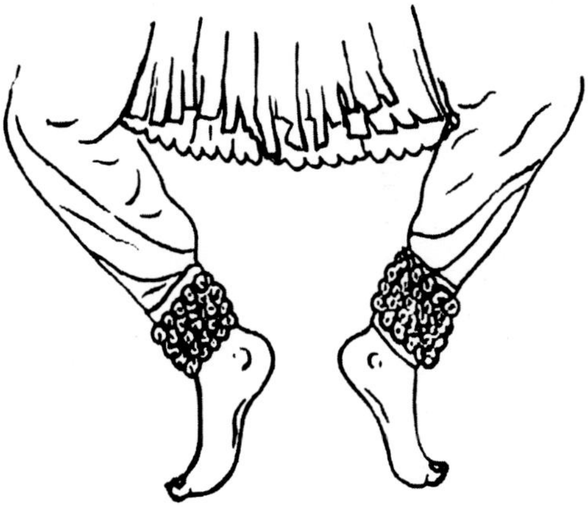

KUDITTU ADAVU

CHAPTER-3

HASTA–MUDRA

Gestures played an important role in communication among the primitive people. Even now, gestures are used when the language barrier comes and some of the emotions cannot be expressed without the hand movements. When these hand gestures form difinite patterns systematically and artistically and are adopted in dance, they called *hastas* and *mudras.*

Bharata Natyam is unique in its emphasis on facial expressions, particularly when the dance seeks to depict the substance of a song. Such *abhinaya* is supported by the *hastas* and *mudras.*

According to the followers of the *tantrik* school, a *mudra* is a symbolic representation of a person, place or thing, through the manner in which the palms, the thumbs and the fingers are arranged in different formations. The *hasta* is classified as *asamyuta* and *samyuta* depending on whether one hand is used or both. Similarly *mudras* can be formed with one or both hands, each *mudra* having a separate significance or meaning. The dancer therefore synchronises the facial expressions with the *hasta* and the *mudra* to portray the particular item or items mentioned in the song.

Symmetry and balance being the *forte* of *Bharata Natyam,* the *hastas* (as also the movements of the head, the neck and the eyes) go along with the *adavus* in footwork to give the picture of completeness.

However, certain selected *hastas* alone are employed alongwith the footwork while dancing the pure *nritta* sequences or items and these hastas are therefore referred to as *nritta-hastas. Patāka, tripatāka, katakāmukha, alapadma, shikhara, dola, chatura, tāmrachooda* etc., are such decorative *hastas* which, while displayed alongwith *adavus* do not signify any meaning, but help edify the execution of the *adavus.*

हस्तभेदाः

अथेदानीं तु हस्तानां लक्षणं प्रोच्यते मया।।
असंयुताः संयुताश्च हस्ताःद्वेधा निरुपिताः।
तत्रासंयुतहस्तानामादौ लक्षणमुच्यते।।

असंयुतहस्ताः

पताकस्त्रिपताकोऽर्धपताकः कर्तरीमुखः।
मयूराख्योऽर्धचन्द्रश्चारालः शुकतुण्डकः।।
मुष्टिश्च शिखराख्यश्च कपित्थः कटकामुखः।
सूची चन्द्रकला पद्मकोशः सर्पशिरस्त था।।
मृगशीर्षः सिंहमुखः काङ्गुलश्चालपद्मकः।
चतुरो भ्रमरश्चैव हंसास्यो हंसपक्षकः।।
सन्दंशो मुकुलश्चैव ताम्रचूडस्त्रिशूलकः।
इत्यसंयुतहस्तानामष्टाविंशतिरीरिता।।

संयुतहस्ताः

अञ्जलिश्च कपोतश्च कर्कटः स्वस्तिकस्तथा।
डोलाहस्तः पुष्पपुट उत्सङ्गः शिवलिङ्गकः।।
कटकावर्धनश्चैव कर्तरीस्वस्तिकस्तथा।
शकटं शङ्खचक्रे च संपुटः पाशकीलकौ।।
मत्स्यः कूर्मो वराहश्च गरुडो नागबन्धकः।
खट्वा भेरुण्ड इत्येते संख्याताः संयुताः कराः।।
त्रयोविंशतिरित्युक्ताः पूर्वगैर्भरतादिभिः।

ASAMYUTA

1. Patāka 2. Tripatāka 3. Ardhapatāka 4. Kartareemukha 5. Mayura 6. Ardha Chandra 7. Arāla 8. Shukatunda 9. Mushti 10. Shikhara 11. Kapittha 12. Katakāmukha 13. Soochi 14. Chandrakalā 15. Padmakosha 16. Sarpasheersha 17. Mrugasheersha 18. Simha Mukha 19. Kāngula 20. Alapadma 21. Chatura 22. Bhramara 23. Hamsāsya 24. Hamsapaksha 25. Sandamsha 26. Mukula 27. Tāmrachooda 28. Trishula

Certain other *asamyuta hastas* like *vyaghra* and *ardhasoochi* have also come into common usage.

SAMYUTA

1. Anjali 2. Kapota 3. Karkata 4. Svastika 5. Dolā 6. Pushpaputa 7. Utsanga 8. Shivalinga 9. Katakā Vardhana 10. Kartareesvastika 11. Shakata 12. Shankha 13. Chakra 14. Samputa 15. Pasha 16. Keelaka 17. Matsya 18. Koorma 19. Varāha 20. Garuda 21. Naga-bandha 22. Khatva 23. Bherunda

1. PATĀKA

Four fingers stretched close together with a bent thumb.

Beginning of dance, blessings, destroying or slashing, waves, wind etc.

पताकहस्तः
अङ्गुल्य कुश्चिताङ्गुष्ठः संश्लिष्टाः प्रसृता यदि।
स पताककरः प्रोक्तो नृत्यकर्मविशारदैः।।

2. TRIPATĀKA

Assume Pataka hasta and bend the ring finger at the second phalange from the top.

Sun, season, crown, light, tree, pigeon, fire etc.

त्रिपताकहस्तः
स एव त्रिपताकः स्याद्वक्रितानामिकाङ्गुलिः।।

3. ARDHA PATĀKA

Adopt Tripatāka hasta and bend the little finger also along with the ring finger.

Two persons, bank of a river, tower, flag, etc.

अर्धपताकहस्तः
त्रिपताके कनिष्ठा चेद् वक्रिताऽर्धपताकिका।

4. KARTAREEMUKHA

Adopt Ardhapataka hasta and take the index finger backward and the middle finger slightly forward.

Death, lightning, hatred, scissors, breaking, reverse etc.

कर्तरीमुखहस्तः
अस्यैव चापि हस्तस्य तर्जनी च कनिष्ठिका।
बहिः प्रसारिते द्वे च स करः कर्तरीमुखः।।

5. MAYURA

Adopt Patāka hasta and let thumb and ring fingers touch the tips of each other.

Peacock, flag, tresses etc.

मयूरहस्तः
अस्मिन्ननामिकाङ्गुष्ठौ श्लिष्टौ चान्याः प्रासारिताः।
मयूरहस्तः कथितः करटीकाविचक्षणैः।।

6. ARDHA CHANDRA

Adopt the Pataka hasta and stretch the thumb outward and four fingers pointing sidewards, palm facing the body and the thumb up.

Half moon, waist pushing etc.

अर्धचन्द्रहस्तः
अर्धचन्द्रकरः सोऽयं पताकेऽङ्गुष्ठसारणात्।

7. ARĀLA

Adopt the Pataka hasta and bend the index finger such that the tip of the thumb touches the middle phalange of the index finger.

Poison, meditation, prasadam etc.

अरालहस्तः
पताके तर्जनी वक्रा नाम्ना सोऽयमरालकः ।

8. SHUKATUNDA

The index and the ring fingers should be folded in Pataka hasta or the ring finger should also be bent in the Arāla Hasta.

Feeling, aiming the arrow, secret etc.

शुकतुण्डहस्तः
अस्मिन्ननामिका वक्रा शुकतुण्डकरो भवेत् ।

9. MUSHTI

All the four fingers should be folded and thumb placed on them.

Valour, catching hold of something like saree, hair or plait and pulling it etc.

मुष्टिहस्तः
मेलनादङ्गुलीनाञ्च कुञ्चितानां तलान्तरे ।
अङ्गुष्ठश्चोपरियुतो मुष्टिहस्तोऽयमीर्यते ।।

10. SHIKHARA

The thumb should be stretched up in the Mushti hasta.

Lips, bow, embraces, leader, questions, ringing the bell etc.

शिखरहस्तः
चेन्मुष्टिरुन्नताङ्गुष्ठः स एव शिखरः करः।।

11. KAPITTHA

The index finger should be curved up to touch the tip of the thumb in the Shikara hasta.

Goddess, lady, holding the stick or cane, milking the cow etc.

कपित्थहस्तः
अङ्गुष्ठमूर्धनि शिखरे वक्रिता यदि तर्जनी।
कपित्थारव्यंः करः सोऽयं कीर्तितो नृत्यकोविदैः।।

12. KATAKĀ MUKHA

(i) The middle finger is also bent with the index finger in the Kapitthā hasta.

(ii) The thumb, the index and the middle fingers are joined together straight and the last two fingers are spread out.

Plucking flowers, stretching the bow, pouring liquid, catching the container etc.

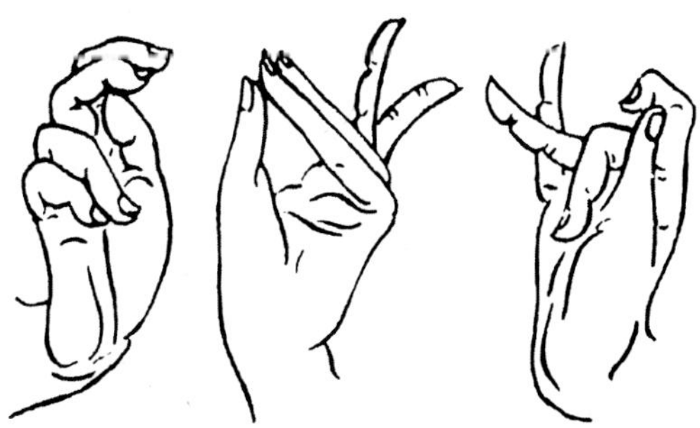

कटकामुखहस्तः
कपित्थे तर्जनी चोध्वधर्वमुच्छ्रिताङ्गुष्ठमध्यमा।
कटकामुखहस्तोऽयं कथितो भरतागमैः।।

13. SOOCHI

The index finger is stretched straight to point upward in the Katakāmukha hasta.

One, that, you, world, universe, umbrella etc.

सूचीहस्तः
ऊर्ध्वप्रसारिता यत्र कटकामुखतर्जनी।
सूचीहस्तः स विज्ञेयो भरतागमकोविदैः।।

14. CHANDRA KALĀ

The thumb should be stretched outward in the Soochi hasta.

Ganges on Shiva's head, face, surprise etc.

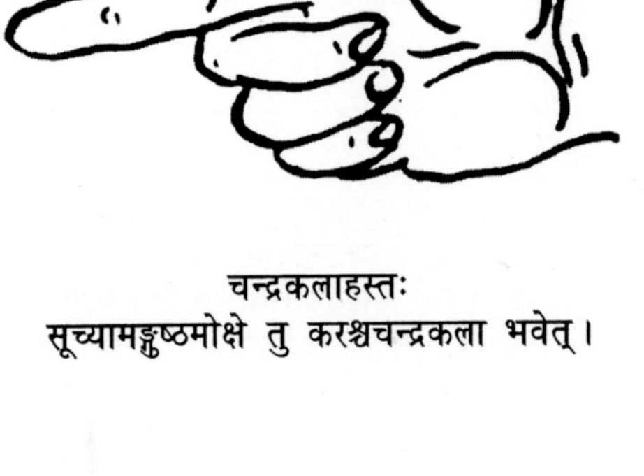

चन्द्रकलाहस्तः
सूच्यामङ्गुष्ठमोक्षे तु करश्चचन्द्रकला भवेत्।

15. PADMAKOSHA

All the fingers are stretched and brought close but not touching one another.

Flower buds, fruits, butter, small article, stone etc.

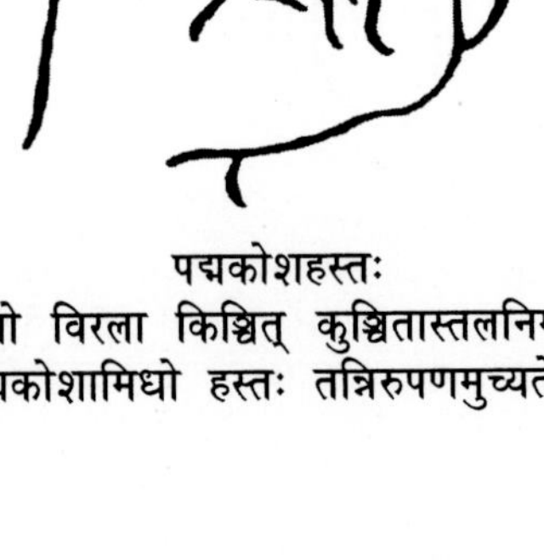

पद्मकोशहस्तः
अङ्गुल्यो विरला किञ्चित् कुञ्चितास्तलनिमन्गाः।
पद्मकोशामिधो हस्तः तन्निरुपणमुच्यते।।

16. SARPASHEERSHA

The tips of the fingers are curved in Pataka hasta.

Snakes head, elephant's head, protection etc.

सर्पशीर्षहस्तः
पताका नमिताग्रा चेत् सर्पशीर्षकरो भवेत् ।।

17. MRUGASHEERSHA

Either in the sarpsheersha hasta, the little finger and the thumb are straightened or in the patāka hasta, the middle three fingers are stretched and bent forward and the thumb stretched outward.

Calling, hearing, cheeks, dress, deer etc.

मृगशीर्षहस्तः
अस्मिन् कनिष्ठिकाङ्गुष्ठे प्रसृते मृगशीर्षकः ।

18. SIMHA MUKHA

The middle and the ring finger are bent forward to touch the thumb in Pataka hasta.

Deer, cow, bull, throne, yagna etc.

सिंहमुखहस्तः
मध्यमानामिकाग्राभ्यामङ्गुष्ठो मिश्रितो यदि ।
शेषै प्रसारितौ यत्र स सिंहास्यकरो भवेत् ।।

19. KĀNGULA

The ring finger is curved inside in Padmakosha hasta.

A small fruit, lily bell, any small thing, cocoanut etc.

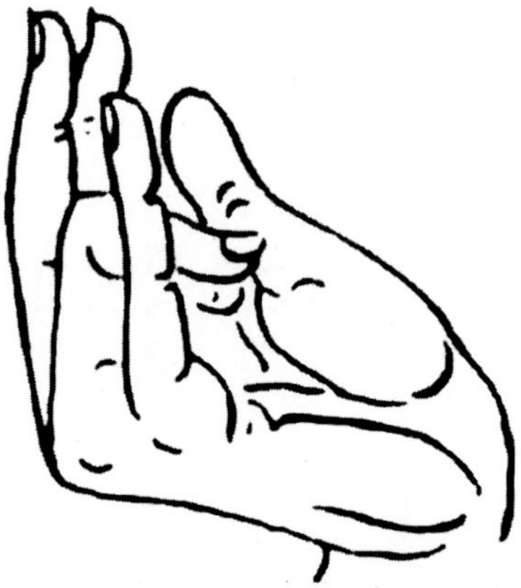

काङ्गुलहस्तः
पद्मकोशेऽनामिका चेन्नम्रा काङ्गुलहस्तकः ।।

20. ALAPADMA

All fingers stretched apart and the index finger stretched straight and the little finger bent inward.

Flower, all, sky, wheel, lotus, fruits, pangs of separation, full moon, pride etc.

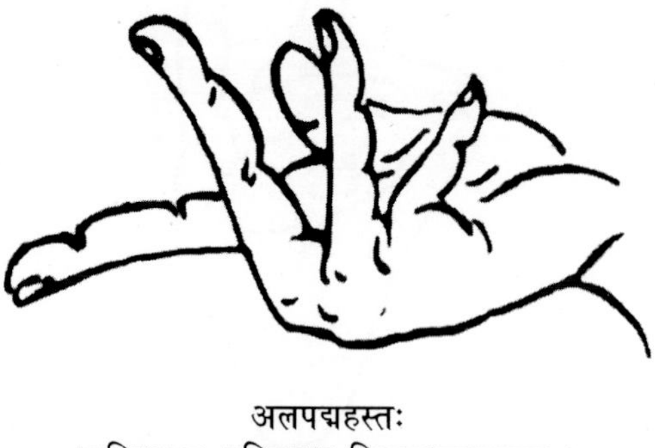

अलपद्महस्तः
कनिष्ठाद्या वक्रिताश्च विरलाश्चालपद्मकः ।

21. CHATURA

The little finger is straight down, the other three fingers bent upwards with the thumb curved to touch the three middle fingers.

Square, small or little, steps, friendships etc.

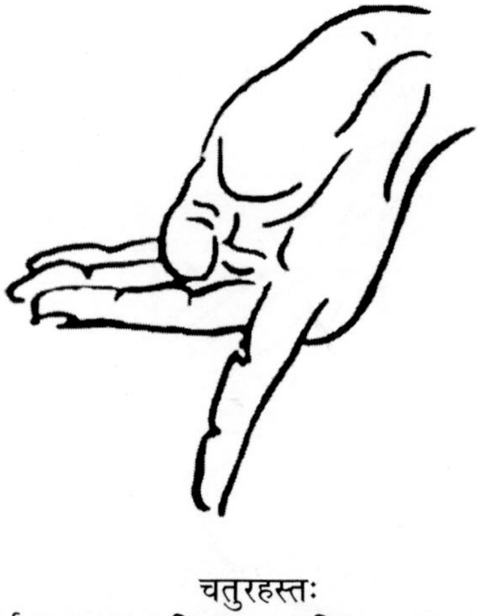

चतुरहस्तः
तर्जन्याद्यास्तत्र श्लिष्टाः कनिष्ठा प्रसृता यदि
अङ्गुष्ठोऽनामिकामूले तिर्यक् चेच्चतुरः करः ।।

22. BHRAMARA

The middle finger and the thumb should touch each other, the finger being curved and the last two fingers stretched.

Bee, Male lover etc.

भ्रमरहस्तः
मध्यमाङ्गुष्ठसंयोगे तर्जनी वक्रिताकृतिः।
शेषा प्रसारिताश्चासौ भ्रमराभिधहस्तकः।।

23. HAMSASYA

The first finger stretched to touch the thumb with the other three fingers stretched straight.

Writing, crying, preaching etc.

हंसास्यहस्तः
मध्यमाद्यास्त्रयोऽङ्गुल्यः प्रसृता विरला यदि।
तर्जन्यङ्गुष्ठसंश्लेषात् करो हंसास्यको भवेत्।।

24. HAMSAPAKSHA

Keep the little finger straight in sarpasheersha hasta.

Bridge, number six, vehicles, nailmarks etc.

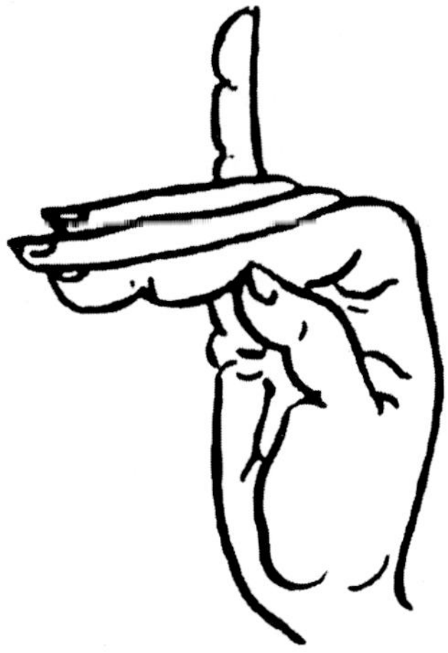

हंसपक्षहस्तः
सर्पशीर्षकरे सम्यक् कनिष्ठा प्रसृता यदि।
हंसपक्षकरः सोऽयं तन्निरुपणमुच्यते।।

25. SANDAMSHA

The fingers are moved up and down in a vibrating motion in the Padmakosha hasta.

Five, heart-beat, prayer with flowers, worms, fear etc.

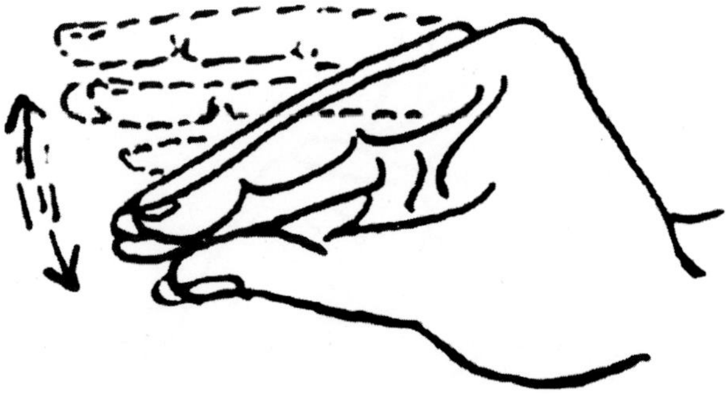

सन्दंशहस्तः
पुनः पुनः पद्मकोशः संश्लिष्टो विरलो यदि।
सन्दंशाभिधहस्तोऽयं कीर्तितो नृत्यकोविदैः।।

26. MUKULA

The tips of all the fingers and the thumb touch one another in a bud formation.

Cupid's arrows, the tender bud, food etc.

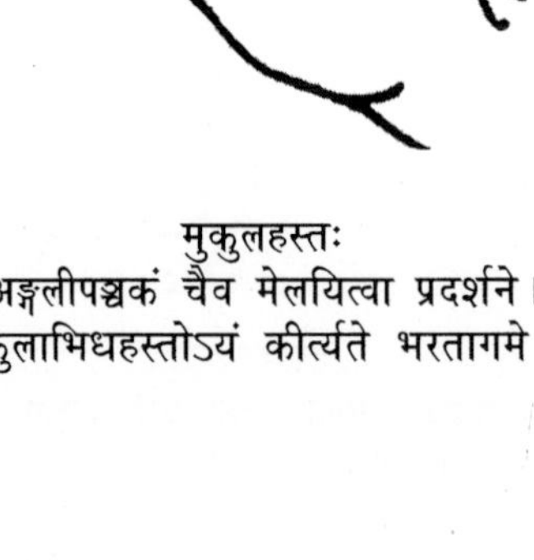

मुकुलहस्तः
अङ्गलीपञ्चकं चैव मेलयित्वा प्रदर्शने।
मुकुलाभिधहस्तोऽयं कीर्त्यते भरतागमे।।

27. TĀMRACHOODA

The index finger is curved up in the Mukula hasta.

Hen, crow, writing etc.

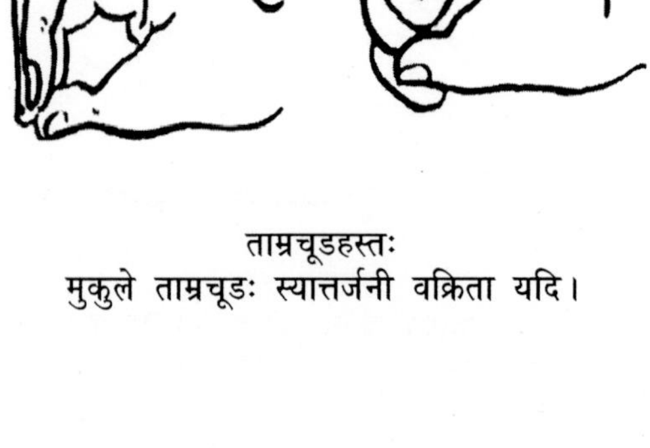

ताम्रचूडहस्तः
मुकुले ताम्रचूडः स्यात्तर्जनी वक्रिता यदि।

28. TRISHULA

The three middle fingers are kept straight pointing upwards with the last finger and the thumb touching each other.

Trishul, three, apply Vibhuti (ash) on the body etc.

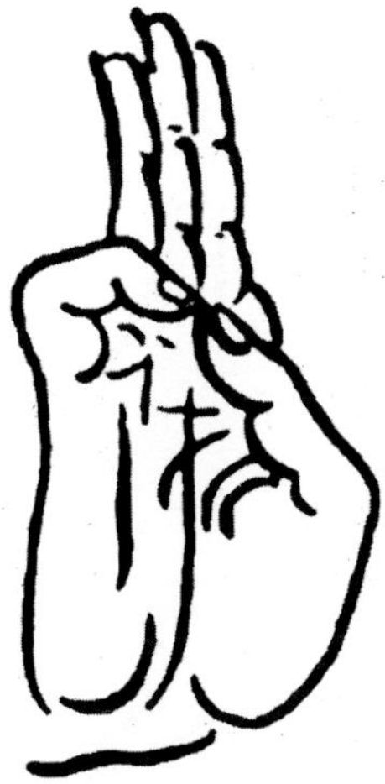

त्रिशूलहस्तः
निकुञ्चनयुताङ्गुष्ठकनिष्ठस्तु त्रिशूलकः।

29. VYAGHRA

The fingers are kept apart in a curved position.

Palm of tiger, monkey, attack by animal etc.

व्याघ्रहस्तः
कनिष्ठाङ्गुष्ठनमने मृगशीर्षकरे तथा।
व्याघ्रहस्तः स विज्ञेयो भरतागमकोविदैः।।

30. ARDHA SOOCHI

In the Kapittha hasta, the index finger is stretched upwards.

Sprouting, worm etc.

अर्धसूचीहस्तः
कपित्थे तर्जनी ऊर्ध्वसारणे त्वर्धसूचिकः।

1. ANJALI

Both hands are joined in patāka hasta.

Prayer to God, obeisance to Guru and elders, welcoming friends and guests etc.

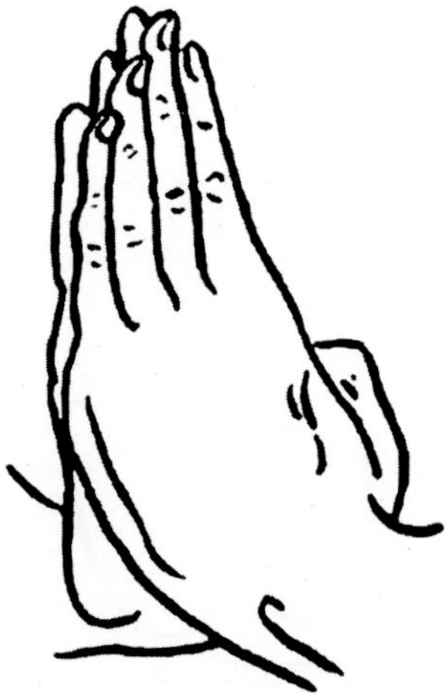

अञ्जलिहस्तः
पताकातलयोर्योगादञ्जलिः करः ईरितः।

2. KAPOTA

The palms are curved outside in Anjali hasta.

Pigeon, lotus, obedient, begging etc.

कपोतहस्तः
कपोतोऽसौ करो यत्र श्लिष्टाऽऽमूलाग्रपार्श्वकः।।

3. KARKATA

The fingers of the two hands cross each other in Anjali hasta and the two wrists are kept apart.

Crowd, awakening from a sleep, friendship, intimacy etc.

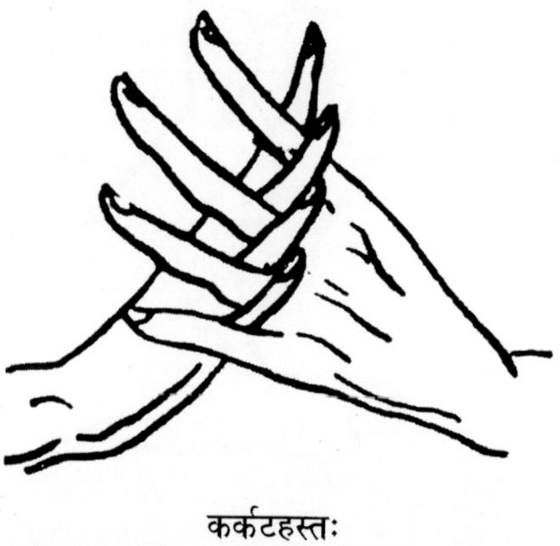

कर्कटहस्तः
अन्योन्यस्यान्तरे यत्राङ्गुल्यो निःसृत्य हस्ययोः।
अन्तर्बहिर्वा वर्तन्ते कर्कटः सोऽभिधीयते।।

4. SVASTIKA

The two hands in pataka hasta cross each other near the wrist and are held slightly apart from each other.

Refusal, fear, crocodile etc.

स्वस्तिकहस्तः
पताकयोः सन्नियुक्तः करयोर्मणिबन्धयोः।
संयोगेन स्वस्तिकाख्यो।।

5. DOLĀ

The hands in front are stretched down with in the patakā hasta.

Swing, big container, percussion instrument like Mrudangam etc.

डोलाहस्तः
पताक ऊरुदेशस्थे डोलाहस्तोऽयमिष्यते।।

6. PUSHPAPUTA

The two hands in Sarpaseersha hasta are joined with the palms facing upwards.

Bhiksha, beg, carry, aarati etc.

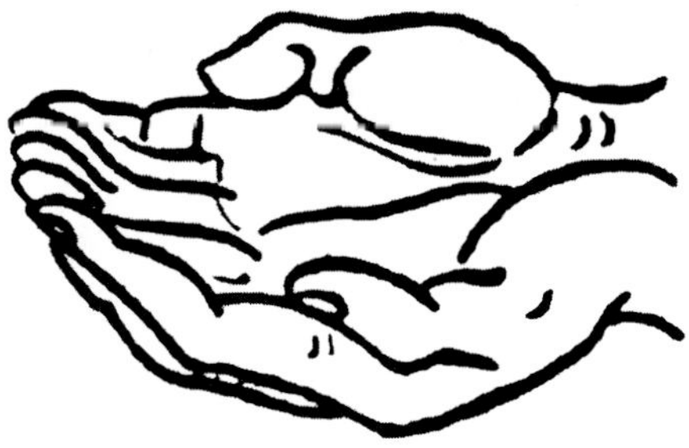

पुष्पपुटहस्तः
संश्लिष्टकरयोः सर्पशीर्षः पुष्पपुटः करः।।

7. UTSANGA

The two hands in Mrugaseersha hasta, facing each other.

Embrace, good relations, growth etc.

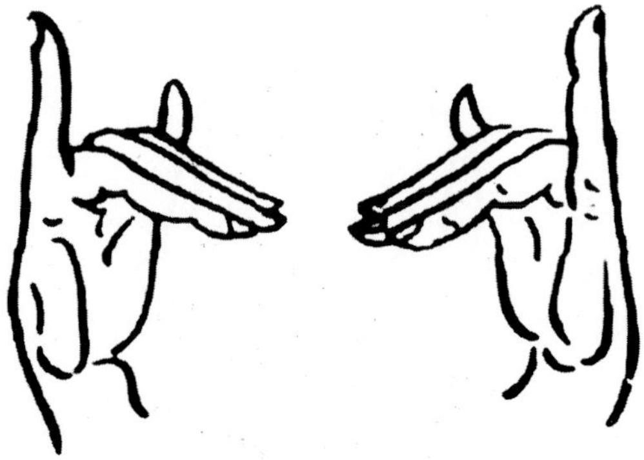

उत्सङ्गहस्तः
अन्योन्यबाहुदेशस्थौ मृगशीर्षकरौ यदि।
उत्सङ्गहस्तः स ज्ञेयो भरतागमवेदिभिः।।

8. SHIVA-LINGA

The left hand in Ardha Chandra hasta with the palm facing upward and the right hand in Shikhara hasta, placed on the left palm.

Shiva-linga, great, chief, authority etc.

शिवलिङ्गहस्तः
वामेऽर्धचन्द्रो विन्यस्तः शिखरः शिवलिङ्गकः।

9. KATAKĀ VARDHANA

The two hands in Katakā hasta are crossed near the wrist.

Pattabhishekam, agreement, union etc.

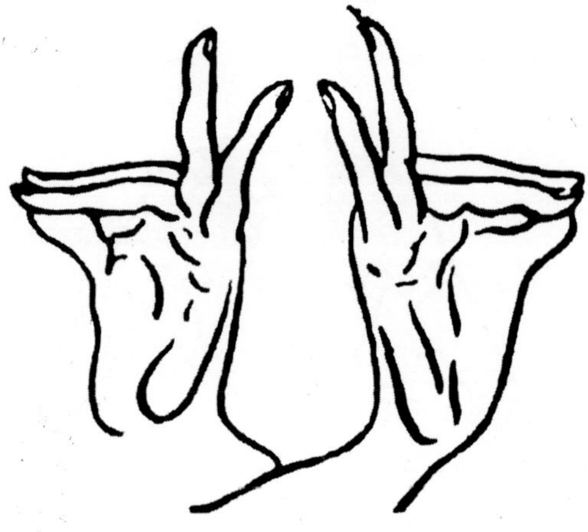

कटकावर्धनहस्तः
कटकामुखयोः पाण्योः स्वस्तिको मणिबन्धयोः।
कटकावर्धनाख्यः स्यादिति नाट्यविदो विदुः।।

10. KARTAREE SVASTIKA

The two hands in Kartaree mukha hasta are crossed near the wrist.

Trees, branches, hills, mountains etc.

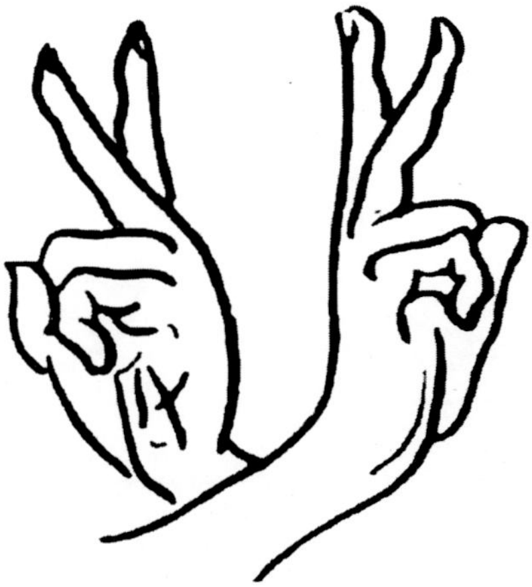

कर्तरीस्वस्तिकहस्तः
कर्तरी स्वस्तिकाकारा कर्तरीस्वस्तिको भवेत् ।।

11. SHAKATA

The two hands in Bhramara hasta (but without joining the thumb and the middle finger) and the hands placed one above the other near the wrist.

Cart, rath (chariot) etc.

शकटहस्तः
भ्रमरे मध्यमाङ्गुष्ठप्रसाराच्छकटो भवेत् ।।

12. SHANKHA

The right hand in Shikhara hasta enclosing the left thumb and four fingers of the left hand touching the right hand.

Conch, heralding the war, prayer.

शङ्खहस्तः
शिखरान्तर्गताङ्गुष्ठ इतराङ्गुष्ठसङ्गत ।
तर्जन्या युत आश्लिष्टः शङ्खहस्तः प्रकीर्तितः ।।

13. CHAKRA

The two hands in Ardha chandra hasta are brought together with the palms facing each other at right angle.

Wheel, Vishnu's chakra etc.

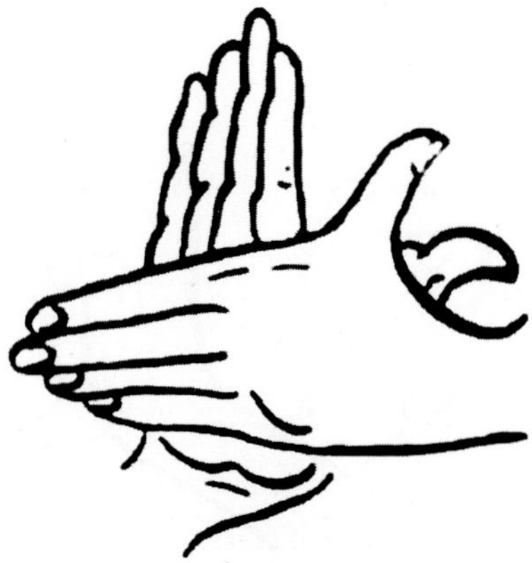

चक्रहस्तः
यत्रार्धचन्द्रौ तिर्यञ्चावन्योन्यतलसंस्पृशौ।
चक्रहस्तः स विज्ञेयः।।

14. SAMPUTA

All the fingers bent forward and the palms kept apart in the Chakra hasta.

Container, closing, playing dice etc.

सम्पुटहस्तः
कुञ्चिताङ्गुलयश्चक्रे प्रोक्तः सम्पुटहस्तकः।

15. PASHA

The index fingers of both the hands in Soochi hasta are curved and interlocked in opposite direction.

Friendship, tie, love, rope etc.

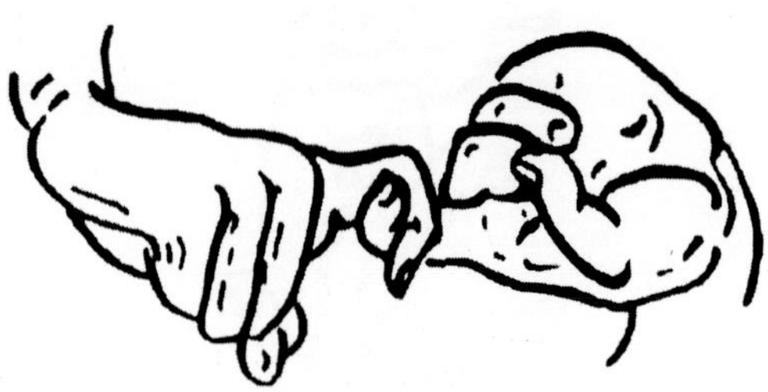

पाशहस्तः
सून्यां निकुञ्चिते श्लिष्टे तर्जन्यौ पाश ईरितः।

16. KEELAKA

In Mrugasheersha hasta the little fingers are curved and interlocked in opposite direction.

Fight, separation etc.

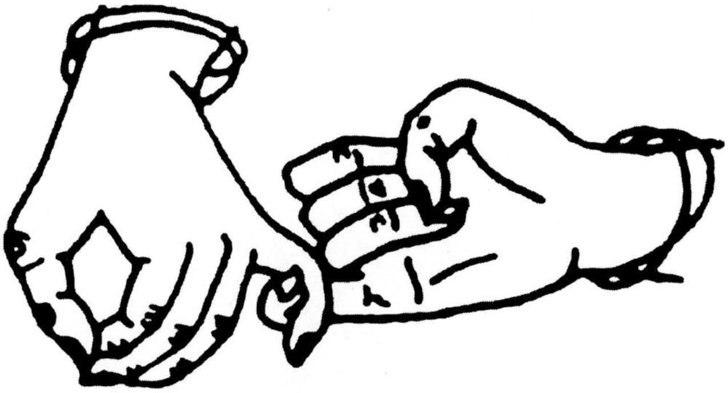

कीलकहस्तः
कनिष्ठे कुञ्चिते श्लिष्टे मृगशीर्षस्तु कीलकः।

17. MATSYA

The two hands in Patāka hasta are placed one above the other with the thumbs pointing outwards.

Fish, Matsya avatar etc.

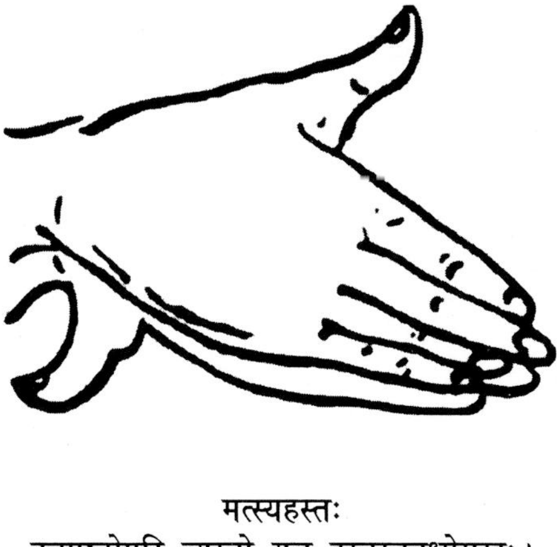

मत्स्यहस्तः
करपृष्टोपरि न्यस्तो यत्र हस्तस्तवधोमुखः।
किञ्चित्प्रसारिताङ्गुष्ठकनिष्ठो मत्स्यनामकः।।

18. KOORMA

The two hands should be in Chakra hasta but with the middle three fingers folded and the little fingers kept straight.

Tortoise, Koorma avatar etc.

कूर्महस्तः
कुञ्चिताग्राङ्गुलिश्चक्रे त्यक्ताङ्गुष्ठकनिष्ठकः।
कूर्महस्तः स विज्ञेयः।।

19. VARĀHA

The two hands in Mrugaseersha hasta should bs placed one above the other with the thumbs and the little fingers stretched out.

Varahha avtar

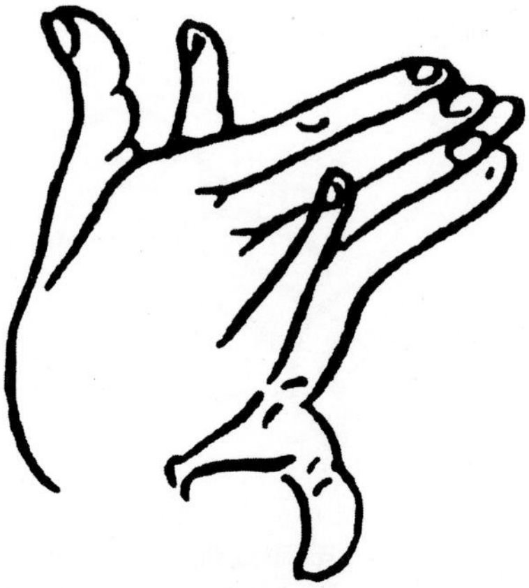

वराहहस्तः
मृगशीर्षे त्वन्यतरे स्वोपर्येकः स्थिते यदि।
कनिष्ठाङ्गुष्ठयोर्योगाद्वराहकर ईरितः।।

20. GARUDA

The palms of the hands in Ardha chandra hasta are kept one above the other with the palms facing the body and the thumbs kept together.

Birds

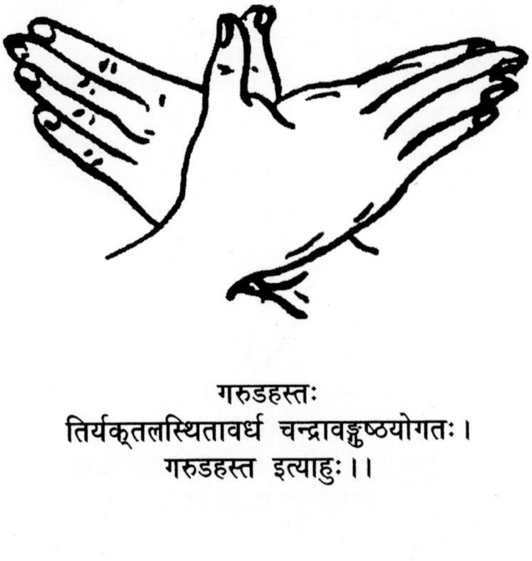

गरुडहस्तः
तिर्यक्तलस्थितावर्ध चन्द्रावङ्गुष्ठयोगतः।
गरुडहस्त इत्याहुः।।

21. NAGA-BANDHA

The two hands in Sarpaseersha hasta are crossed near the wrist.

Snakes.

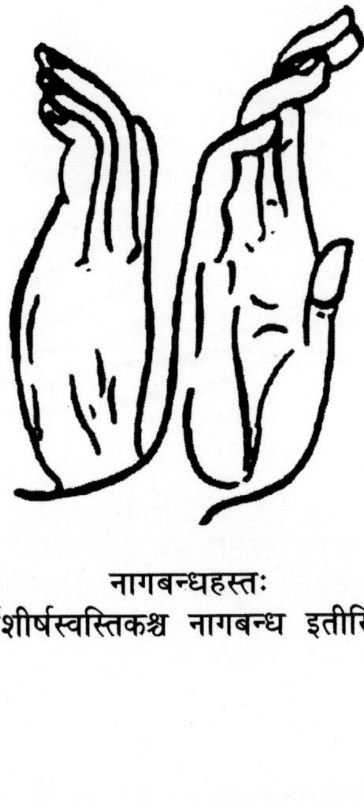

नागबन्धहस्तः
सर्पशीर्षस्वस्तिकश्च नागबन्ध इतीरितः।

22. KHATVA

The two hands in Chatura hasta are joined together with the index fingers and the little fingers pointing straight downwards.

Cot.

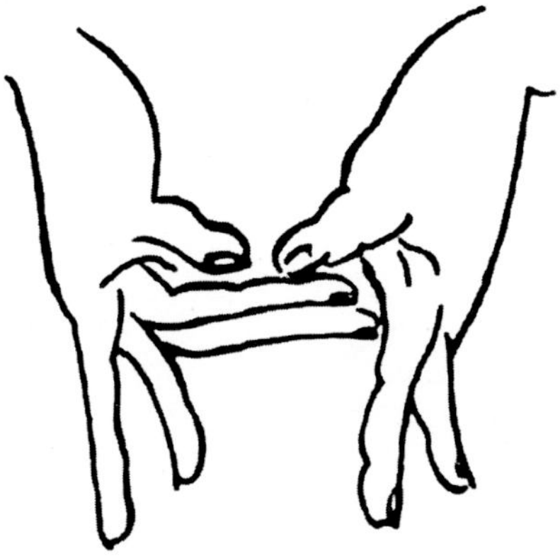

खट्वाहस्तः
चतुरे चतुरं न्यस्य तर्जन्यङ्गुष्ठमोक्षतः।
खट्वाहस्तो भवेदेषः।।

23. BHERUNDA

The two hands in the Kapitta hasta are crossed near the wrist.

Embrace, bherunda etc

भेरुण्डहस्तः
मणिबन्धे कपित्याभ्यां भेरुण्डकर इप्यते।

NAVAGRAHA HASTA

Soorya

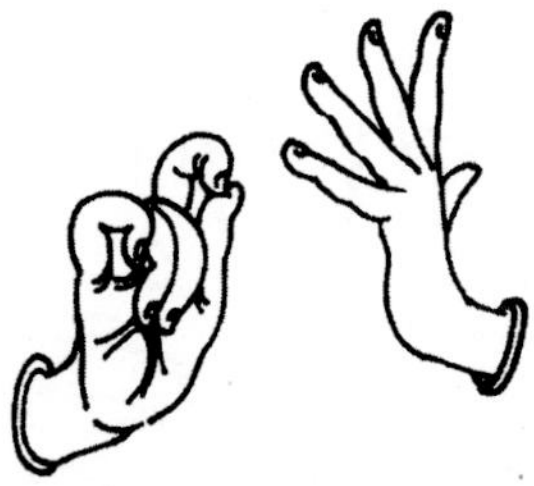

Mangal

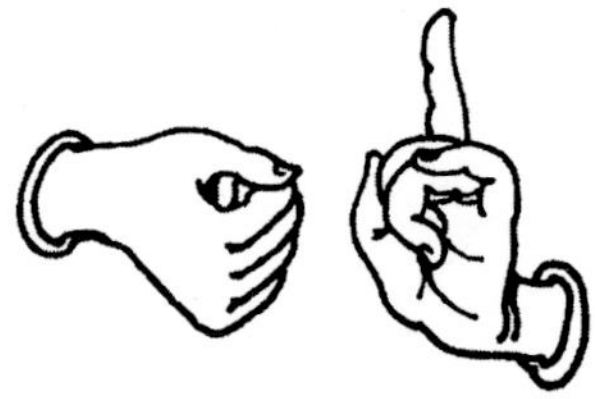

Chandra

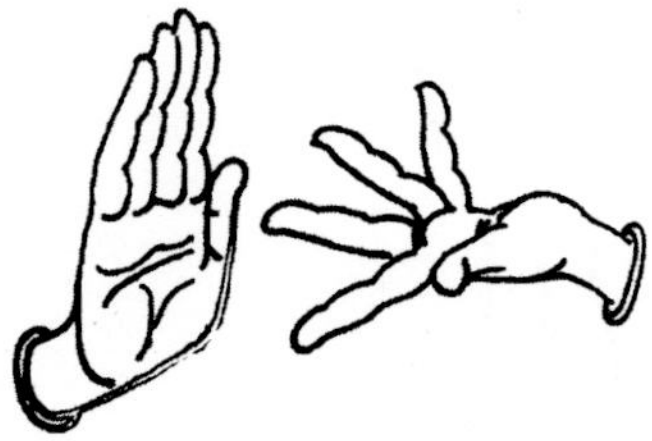

Buddha

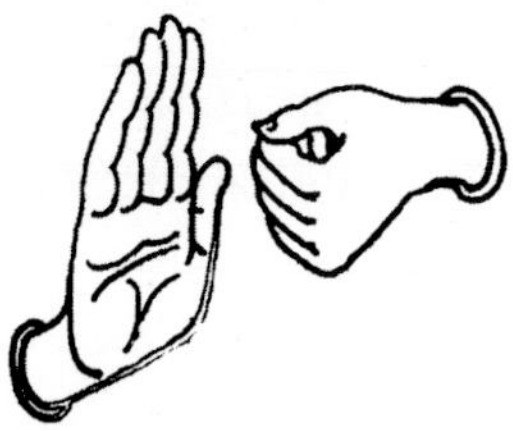

Shukra

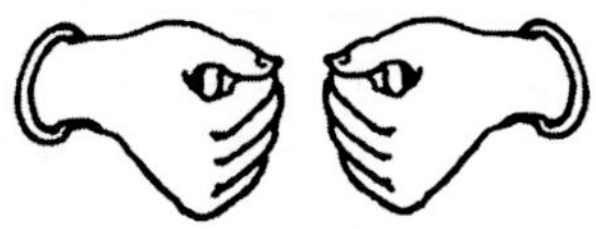

Guru

Rahu

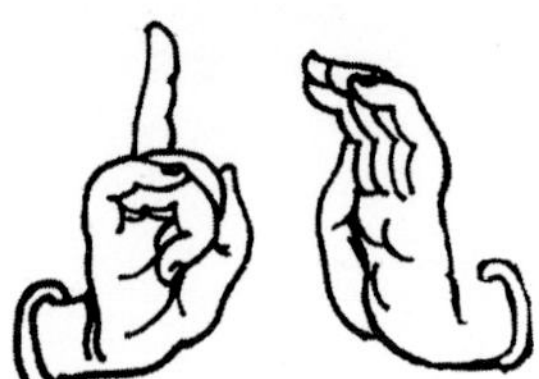

Shani

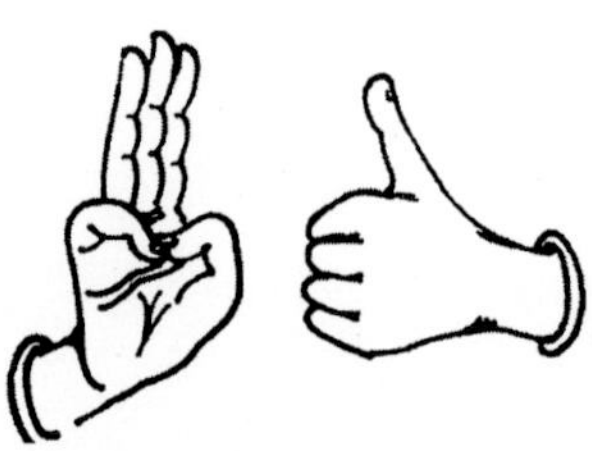

Ketu

DASHAVATAR HASTA

Matsya

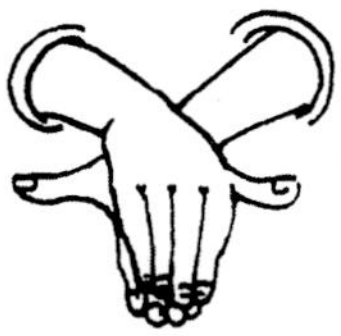

Kurma

Varaha

Narasimha

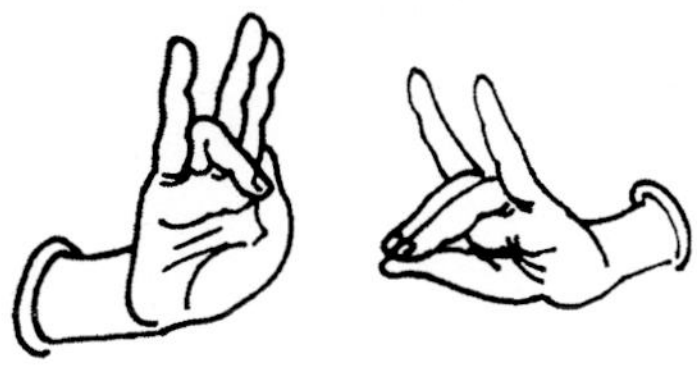

Parashuram

Vamana

Rama

Balarama

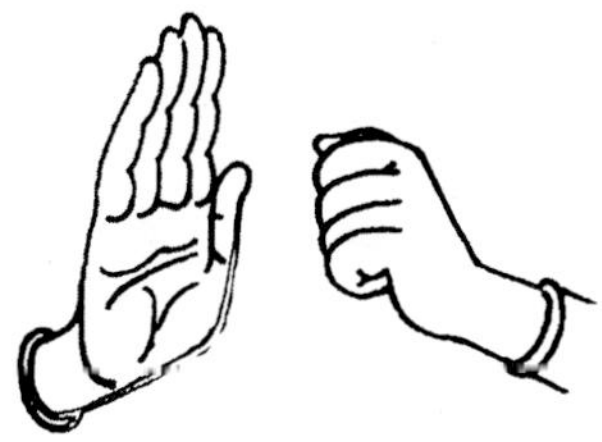

Krishna

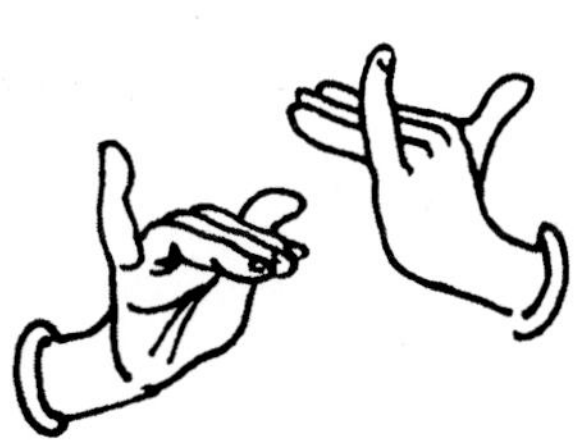

Kalki

CHAPTER-4

BHEDA
(Classification of Movements)

A *Bharata Natyam* dancer seeks, for the most part, to portray the meaning of a composition. The meaning is conveyed by a variety of movements—movements of the head, the eyes, the neck etc. and by different poses assumed with hands and legs. In proper sequence and in appropriate combinations, the movements and poses help to express the essence of the composition. The different varieties of movements are called *bheda*. The movements of the head, the eyes and the neck are respectively known as *shiro-bheda*, *drishti-bheda* and *kantha-bheda*.

The manner of executing the different *bhedas* and their usage are indicated in the following pages.

शिरोभेदाः
सममुद्वाहितमधोमुखमालोलितं धुतम् ।।
कम्पितं च परावृत्तमुत्क्षिप्तं परिवाहितम्
नवधा कथितं शीर्ष नाट्यशास्त्रविशारदैः ।।

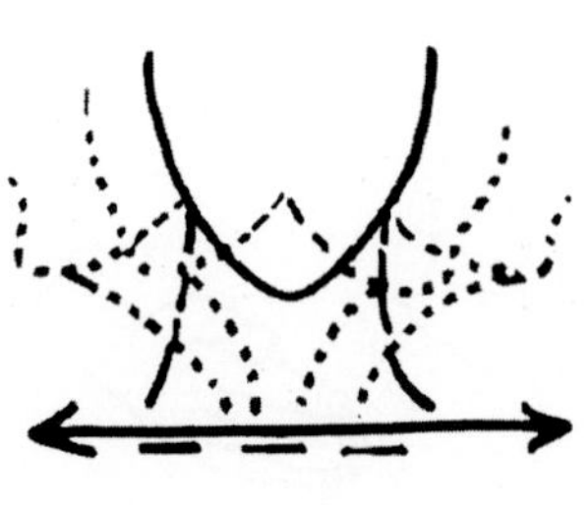

Authorities on the fine art of Bharata Natyam enumerated nine modes of head-movements namely *Sama*, *Udvāhita*, *Adhomukha*, *Ālokita*, *Dhuta*, *Kampita*, *Paravritta*, *Utkshipta and Parivahita*.

SHIRO-BHEDA
(GESTURES BY THE HEAD)

1. SAMA SHIRA

Keep the head straight without any movement.

Beginning of a performance, meditation, anger etc.

समशिरः
निश्चलं सममारव्यातं यन्नत्युन्नतिवर्जितम् ।

2. UDVĀHITA SHIRA

Move the face upwards and keep the head in that position.

Sun, stars, sky, moon, mountain etc.

उद्वाहितशिरः
उद्वाहितशिरो ज्ञेयमूर्ध्वभागोन्नताननम् ।।

3. ADHOMUKHA SHIRA

Move the face downwards and keep the head in that position.

Love, pangs of separation, despair, shyness, respect etc.

अधोमुखशिरः
अधस्तान्नमितं वक्त्रमधोमुखमितीरितम् ।

4. ĀLOLITA SHIRA

Move the head in a circular way.

State of intoxication fainting, laugh with wickedness etc.

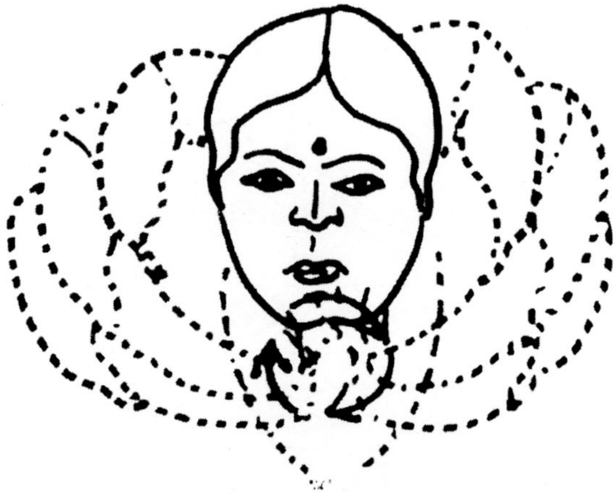

आलोलितशिरः
मण्डलाकारमुद्भ्रान्तमालोलितशिरो भवेत्।

5. DHUTA SHIRA

Move the head from left to right and vice versa.

Refusal, rejection etc.

धुतशिरः
वामदक्षिणभागेषु चलिजं तद्धुतं शिरः।

6. KAMPITA SHIRA

Move the head up and down.

Anger, question, scolding etc.

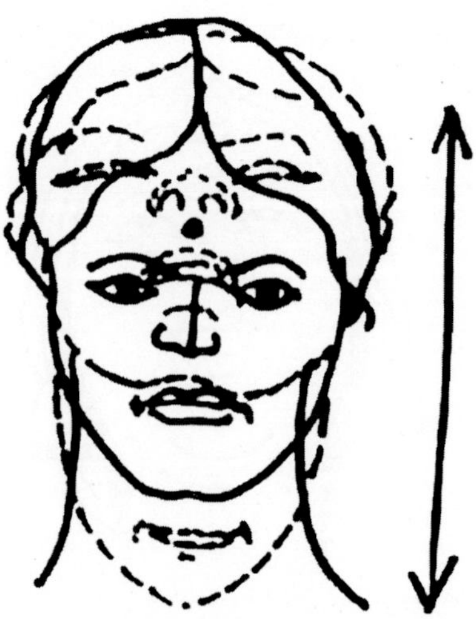

कम्पितशिरः
ऊर्ध्वाधोभागचलितं तच्छिरः कम्पितं भवेत्।

7. PARĀVRITTA SHIRA

Turn the head to one side and look over the shoulder.

Ignoring a proposal looking behind etc.

परावृत्तशिरः
पराङ्मुखीकृतं शीर्ष परावृत्तमितीरितम् ।।

8. UTKSHIPTA SHIRA

Turn the head to one side and look up.

Order something, ask some one to go, command someone etc.

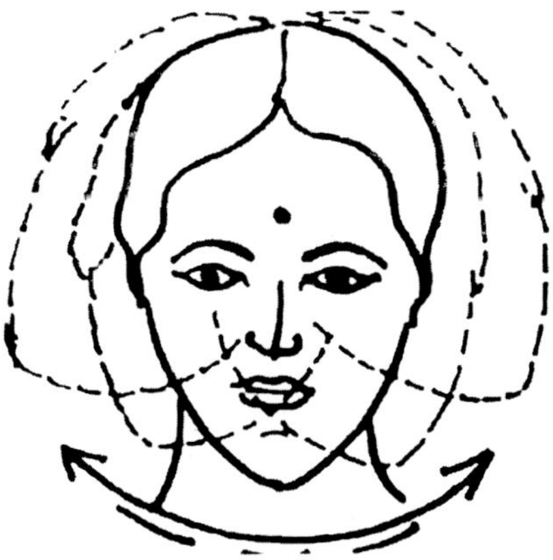

उत्क्षिप्तशिरः
पार्श्वोर्ध्वभागचलितमुत्क्षिप्तं कथ्यते शिरः ।

9. PARIVAHITA SHIRA

Move the head and the neck together from one side to the other.

Love for children, prayer, enjoying music etc.

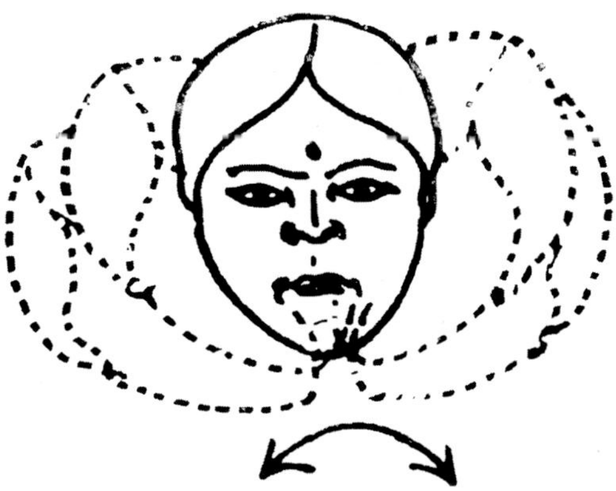

परिवाहितशिरः
पार्श्वयोश्चामरमिव ततं चेत् परिवाहितम् ।

DRISHTI BHEDA OR NETRA BHEDA
(GESTURES THROUGH THE EYES)

दृष्टिभेदाः
सममालोकितं साची प्रालोकितनिमीलिते।
उल्लोकितानुवृत्ते च तथा चैवावलोकितम्।।
इत्यष्टौ दृष्टिभेदाः स्युः कीर्तिताः पूर्वसूरिभिः।

The eight varieties of gestures through the movements of the eyes as identified by the ancient authorities are *Sama, Ālokita, Sāchi, Pralokita, Nimeelita, Ullokita, Anuvrutta* and *Avalokita*

1. SAMA DRISHTI

Keep the eyes open normally without blinking.

The beginning of a recital, concentration etc.

समदृष्टिः
वीक्षितं सुरनारीवत् सानन्दं समवीक्षणम्।।

2. ALOKITA DRISHTI

Open the eyes wide and roll them.

Wonder, surprise, admiration etc.

आलोकितदृष्टिः
आलोकितं भवेदाशुभ्रमणं स्फुटवीक्षणम्।

3. SACHI DRISHTI

Side glance.

Secret admiration or love, aiming with an arrow etc.

साचीदृष्टिः
स्वस्थाने तिर्यगाकारमपाङ्गवलनं क्रमात्।
साचीदृष्टिरिति ज्ञेया नाट्यशास्त्रविशारदैः।।

4. PRALOKITA DRISHTI

Look both sides, one after another.

Addressing a meeting, total view of all the sides etc.

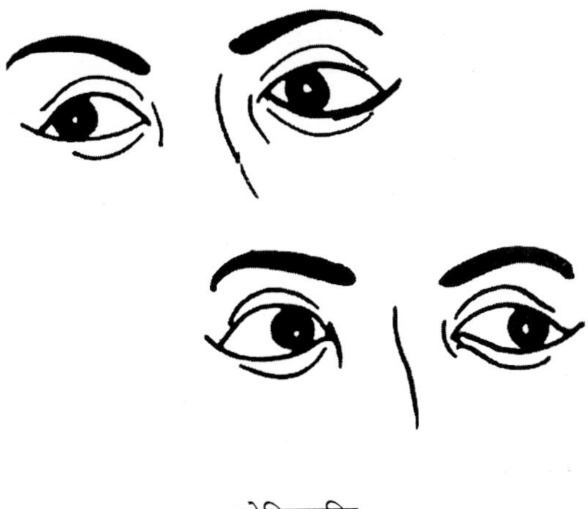

प्रलोकितदृष्टिः
प्रलोकितं परिज्ञेयं चलनं पार्श्वभागयोः।।

5. MEELITA DRISHTI (NIMEELITA)

Keep the eyes half open.

Meditation, prayer, peace, trance, intoxication etc.

मीलितदृष्टिः
दृष्टेरर्धविकासेन मीलिता दृष्टिरीरिता।

6. ULLOKITA DRISHTI

Raise the eyes and look upwards.

Heaven, sky, stars, sun, moon, remembering previous events etc.

उल्लोकितदृष्टिः
उल्लोकितमिति ज्ञेयमूर्ध्वभागे विलोकितम् ।।

7. ANUVRUTTA DRISHTI

Look up and down.

Anger, assessing somebody or admiring etc.

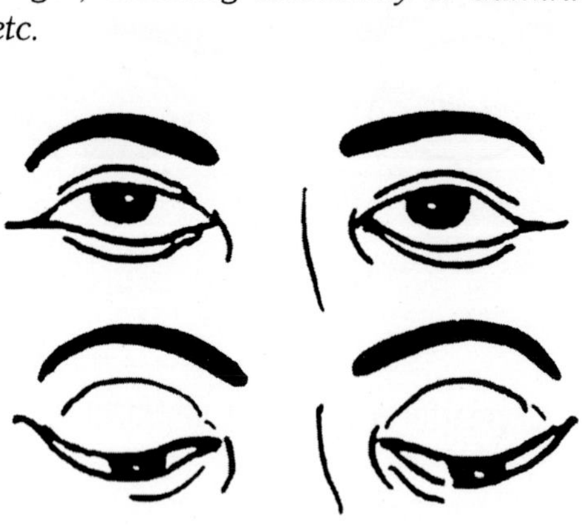

अनुवृत्तदृष्टिः
ऊर्ध्वाधो वीक्षणं वेगादनुवृत्तमितीरितम् ।

8. AVALOKITA DRISHTI

Look downwards.

Shyness, reading or writing, self-admiration etc.

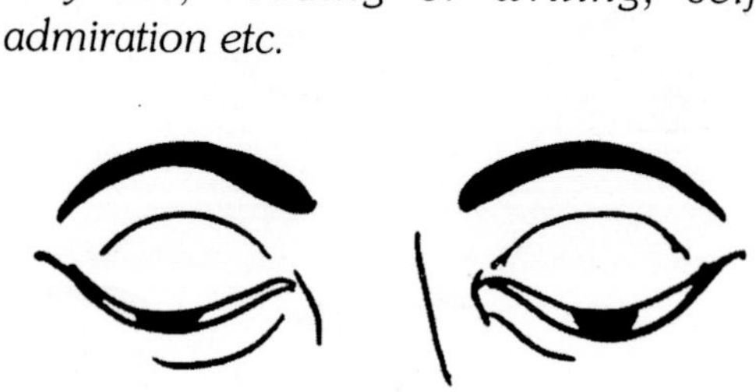

अवलोकितदृष्टिः
अधस्ताद्दर्शनं यत्तदवलोकितमुच्यते ।

KANTHA BHEDA
(MOVEMENTS OF THE NECK)

ग्रीवाभेदाः
सुन्दरी च तिरश्चीना तथैव परिवर्तिता।
प्रकम्पिता च भावज्ञैर्ज्ञेया ग्रीवा चतुर्विधा।।

The movements of the neck have been classified into four kinds namely *Sundari-greeva, Tirascheena-greeva, Parivartita-greeva,* and *Prakampita-greeva.*

1. SUNDARI GREEVA

Move the neck with a slight jerk to the sides and then up and down.

Accepting, listening etc.

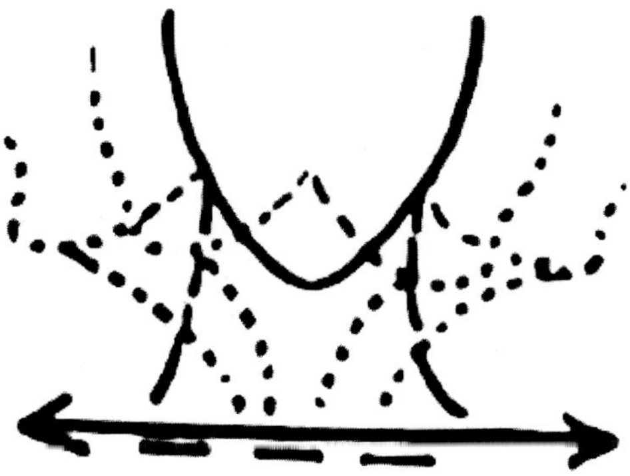

सुन्दरी ग्रीवा
तिर्यक् चञ्चलिता ग्रीवा सुन्दरीति निगद्यते।।

2. TIRASCHEENA GREEVA

Move the neck from one side to the other like the movement of a snake.

Big sword, feeling frustrated and uneasy, snake etc.

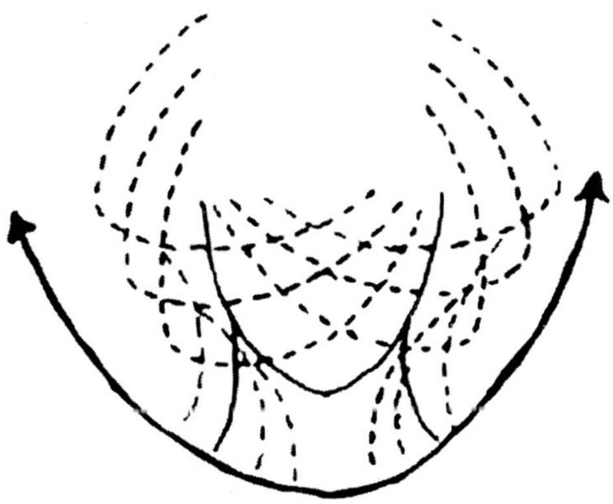

तिरश्चीना ग्रीवा
पार्श्वयोरुर्ध्वभागे तु चलिता सर्पयानवत्।
सा ग्रीवा तु तिरश्चीनेत्युच्यते नाट्यकोविदैः।।

3. PARIVARTITA GREEVA

Move the neck sideways in the form of half moon.

Hearing, whispering love etc.

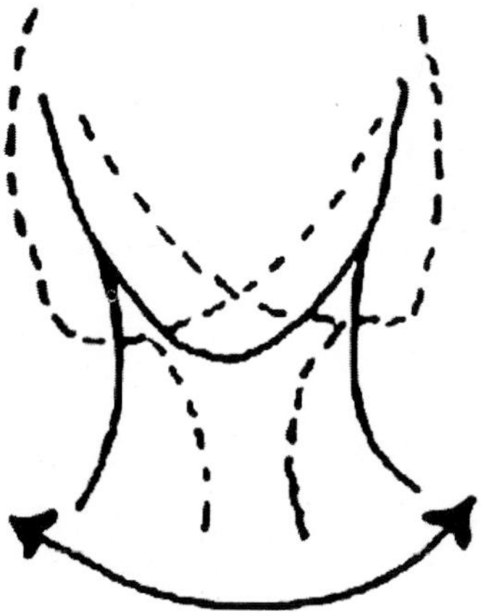

परिवर्तिता ग्रीवा
सव्यापसव्यचलिता ग्रीवा यत्रार्धचन्द्रवत् ।
सा हि नाट्यकलाभिज्ञैर्विज्ञेया परिवर्तिता ।।

4. PRAKAMPITA GREEVA

Move the neck forward and backward like a pigeon.

Yours and mine, swing etc.

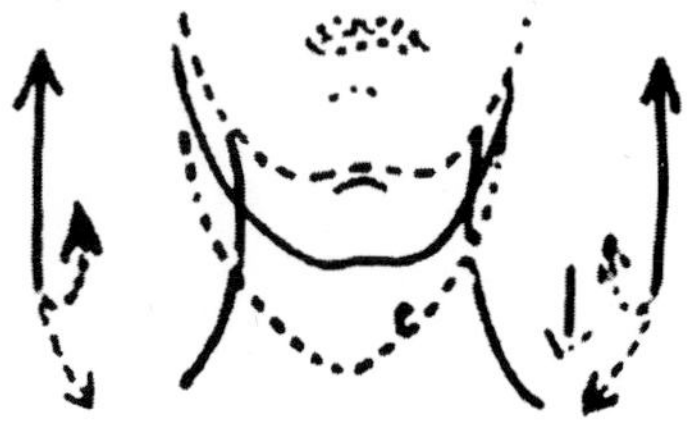

SIDE VIEW

प्रकम्पिता ग्रीवा
पुरः पश्चात्प्रचलनात् कपोतीकण्ठकम्पवत् ।
प्रकम्पितेति सा ग्रीवा नाट्यशास्त्रे प्रशस्यते ।।

CHAPTER-5

ABHINAYA

Facial expressions through *shira, drishti* and *kantha bhedas* are a very essential part of Bharata Natyam

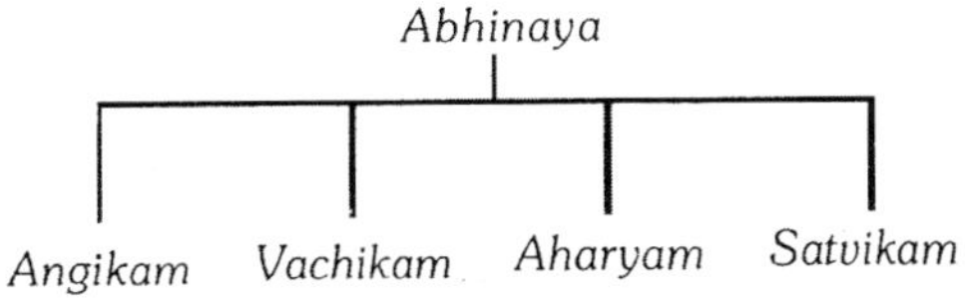

Abhinaya is expressed in four different ways: *Angikabhinaya* (through physical presentation), *Vachikabhinaya* (through verbal or musical presentation), *Aharyabhinaya* (through decorative presentation) and *Satvikabhinaya* (through the evocation of feelings and sentiments). Each form of *Abhinaya* is significant during the portrayal of a concept or while conveying the meaning of the concerned theme to the audience.

नृत्यम्
रसभावव्यञ्जनादियुक्तं नृत्तमितीर्यते ।
एतन्नृत्यं महाराजसभायां कल्पयेत् सदा ।।

Nritya is related to psychological states (bhava) and sentiments (rasas)

Human life is multi-faceted and the people therefore exhibit different emotions at different times depending on the persons and the circumstances that they face. Such emotions, feelings or sentiments have been described as *rasa* of which there are nine. *Bhāva* refers to the expression of such emotions. To be precise, *rasa* refers to the personal experience of emotions by a person while *bhāva* indicates the mimetic expression or display of the emotions by the artiste — the dancer or the actor. *Bhāva* conveys to the spectator or the audience the *rasa* or emotion which the particular character (that the dancer portrays) experiences as per the song. It is a sort of communication by the dancer without herself going through the emotion. But the *bhāva* is so brought out that it transports the spectator to the scene depicted in the song and he or she is able to transcend the present and vibrate in the same wave-length as the character portrayed.

Bhāva has been classified as *sthāyibhāva* and *sanchāribhāva*. *Sthāyi* means permanent and *sanchāri* transitory. In other words, the *sthāyibhāva* denotes the basic emotions or feelings that are lodged in the sub-conscious mind all the time. The *sanchāribhāva* refers to the passing feelings or fleeting sensations. Bharata mentions about eight *sthāyibhāvas:* and, *shamabhāva* representing indifference or neutrality or equanimity is also reckoned as a *sthāyibhāva*. making a total of nine. Correspondingly, there are nine *rasas* as shown below:

स्थायी भावाः

रतिर्हासश्च शोकश्च क्रोधोत्साहौ भयं तथा
जुगुप्सा विस्मयशमाः स्थायी भावा अमी क्रमात् ।।

रसाः

श्रृंगारहास्यकरुणाः रौद्रवीरभयानकाः
बीभत्साद्भुतशान्ताश्च रसाः पूवैरुदाहृताः ।

RASA	STHĀYIBHĀVA
Sringara (Love)	*Rati*
Hāsya (Humour)	*Hāsa*
Karuna (Pity, kindness)	*Shoka*
Roudra (Anger, fury)	*Krodha*
Veera (Valour, heroism)	*Utsāha*
Bhayanaka (Fear)	*Bhaya*
Beebhatsa (Disgust)	*Jugupsā*
Adbhuta (Wonder)	*Vismaya*
Shanta (Tranquillity or contentment)	*Shama (Nirveda)*

Just as the rhythm is maintained by the footwork, and the *mudrās* are executed by the hand gestures, the *bhāva* is expressed through the movements of the eyes, the eye-brows and the lips. For example, *sringara* can be expressed through *adhomukha shira* with *sāchi drishti* and smiling lips. Similarly, *sama shira* with *ālokita drishti* can with raised eyebrows and smiling lips, express *adbhuta* and would, with stiff lips (to give an indication of frown) express *roudra.* Given below is a brief description of the *rasas* and *sthāyibhavas:*

1. *Sringara (Rati):* This stands for romance and romantic love and extends to beauty and beautification. Pangs of separation from the lover are a very important ingredient of this rasa.
2. *Karuna (Shoka):* This means kindness and is often exhibited while fondling a child, petting an animal or soothing someone in distress. This rasa includes an element of pity and sorrow too.
3. *Veera (Utsāha):* This expresses valour or bravery and is associated with the righteous person who destroys the evil and protects the innocent. This portrays generally the triumph of the good over the evil.
4. *Hāsya (Hāsa):* Humour or mirth as normally expressed by an outburst of laughter in a happy or comical situation. It can also be used to express mischief.
5. *Adbhuta (Vismaya):* Surprise at seeing someone or experiencing something unexpected or rare.
6. *Bhayanaka (Bhaya):* The emotion of fear or terror or apprehension.
7. *Beebhatsa (Jugupsā):* The feeling of hatred or disgust or uneasiness or dislike.
8. *Roudra (Krodha):* Anger at being wronged or disappointed or insulted or at disobedience of command.
9. *Shanta (Shama):* Peace, tranquillity or contentment obtained by meditation or by renunciation of worldly desires. Shanta is usually an attribute of Lord Buddha, sages and sanyasis.

SRINGARA (LOVE)

KARUNA (PITY OR KINDNESS)

VEERA (VALOUR)

HASYA (LAUGHTER)

ADBHUTA (SURPRISE)

BHAYA (FEAR)

BEEBHATSA (HATRED)

ROUDRA (ANGER)

SHANTA (PEACE)

CHAPTER-6

TĀLA
(Rhythm-Beat)

कालो मार्गः क्रियांगनि ग्रहोजातिः कळालयः
यतिः प्रस्तारकं चेति ताळप्राणदश स्मृतः ।।

Bharata Natyam has been traditionally based on Karnatic Music — particularly its *tala.* Tala which helps to maintain the time sequence for music, is said to have ten attributes, the more important of which are kriya (action), *anga* (parts), *graha* (starting point), *jaati* (variety), *gati* (duration of beats) *and laya* (speed of rendering).

Kriya means action and in the context of the *tala,* refers to the varieties of movement of the hand for maintaining the *tala.* The well known *kriyas are:*

(a) a beat by the palm — colloquially known as *tattu* in Tamil;

(b) counting of the fingers;

(c) waving of the palm *(veechu* in Tamil) away from the beating position.

Of these, the beat naturally produces some sound and the others do not; the former is technically known as *sashabda* and the latter as *nishabda.*

Anga refers to the parts of the *tala,* each part being made up of one or more of the above *kriyas.* The more widely prevalent *angas* are:

(i) *Anudruta* consisting of just one beat;

(ii) *Druta* consisting of one beat and one *veechu;* and

(iii) *Laghu* consisting of one beat and counting of fingers.

Laghu, anudruta and druta are represented by the symbols I, U, and O (small vertical line, semi-circle and circle respectively) in musical notations.

As indicated earlier, while *anudruta* and *druta* are constant with one and two beats respectively, *laghu* is subject to variation depending on the *jaati* in which it is rendered. Five such *jaatis* (varieties) have been identified such as *tisra, chaturasra, khanda, misra* and *sankeerna,* representing 3,4,5,7 and 9 beats respectively. Thus a *laghu* in *tisra jaati* would consist of three beats, one with sound *(tattu)* and two without sound (counting of fingers). So too, a *laghu* in *misra jaati* would have seven beats of which six would be soundless. The well-known talas of Karnatic Music are described below.

Tala	*Anga-Composition*	*Notation*
Dhruva Tala	Laghu-Druta-Laghu-Laghu	1 0 1 1
Matya Tala	Laghu-Druta-Laghu	1 0 1
Roopaka Tala	Druta-Laghu	0 1
Jampa Tala	Laghu-Anudruta-Druta	1 U 0
Triputa Tala	Laghu-Druta-Druta	1 0 0
Ata Tala	Laghu-Laghu-Druta-Druta	1 1 0 0
Eka Tala	One Laghu only	1

Also, one can straightaway derive 7×5 or 35 talas as shown below:

DHRUVA TALA

Jaati		*Notation*			*Number of Beats*
1. Tisra	l_3	0_2	1_3	l_3	11
2. Chaturasra	1_4	0_2	1_4	1_4	14
3. Khanda	1_5	0_2	1_5	1_5	17
4. Misra	1_7	0_2	1_7	1_7	23
5. Sankeerna	1_9	0_2	I_9	1_9	29

MATYA TALA

Jaati		*Notation*		*Number of Beats*
1. Tisra	1_3	0_2	1_3	8
2. Chaturasra	1_4	0_2	1_4	10
3. Khanda	1_5	0_2	1_5	12
4. Misra	1_7	0_2	1_7	16
5. Sankeerna	1_9	0_2	1_9	20

RUPAKA TALA

Jaati		Notation	Number of Beats
1. Tisra	0_2	1_3	5
2. Chaturasra	0_2	1_4	6
3. Khanda	O_2	1_5	7
4. Misra	0_2	1_7	9
5. Sankeerna	0_2	1_9	11

JAMPA TALA

Jaati		Notation		Number of Beats
1. Tisra	1_3	U_1	0_2	6
2. Chaturasra	1_4	U_1	0_2	7
3. Khanda	1_5	U_1	0_2	8
4. Misra	1_7	U_1	0_2	10
5. Sankeerna	1_9	U_1	0_2	12

TRIPUTA TALA

Jaati		Notation		Number of Beats
1. Tisra	1_3	0_2	0_2	7
2. Chaturasra	1_4	0_2	0_2	8
3. Khanda	1_5	0_2	0_2	9
4. Misra	1_7	0_2	0_2	11
5. Sankeerna	1_9	0_2	0_2	13

ATA TALA

Jaati		Notation			Number of Beats
1. Tisra	1_3	1_3	0_2	0_2	10
2. Chaturasra	1_4	1_4	0_2	0_2	12
3. Khanda	1_5	1_5	0_2	0_2	14
4. Misra	1_7	1_7	0_2	0_2	18
5. Sankeerna	1_9	1_9	0_2	0_2	22

EKA TALA

Jaati	*Notation*	*Number of Beats*
1. Tisra	1_3	3
2. Chaturasra	1_4	4
3. Khanda	1_5	5
4. Misra	1_7	7
5. Sankeerna	1_9	9

Depending on the melodic unit length of the song, the composer chooses an appropriate *tala,* to which he sets the music for his composition.

There is yet another ramification that needs to be mentioned at this juncture. While a beat is normally reckoned as having a unit duration, it is possible to vary the duration of each beat. This variable duration of the beat is referred to as *'gati'* which denotes the flow of music. *Gati* also follows the same classification as *jaati,* namely, *tisra gati, chaturasra gati, khanda gati, misra gati* and *sankeerna gati* representing 3,4,5,7 and 9 unitary durations respectively. A point that needs to be remembered is that while *jaati* (variety) affects *laghu* alone, *gati* (duration of beat) applies to *laghu, druta* as well as *anudruta.*

In this way, it is easy to identify 175 variants of the seven basic *talas.* Let us consider *dhruva tala* to explain the ramifications:—

DHRUVA TALA

Jaati	*Gati*	*Notation of Matras*				
TISRA	1. Tisra	1_{3x3}	0_{2x3}	1_{3x3}	1_{3x3}	33
	2. Chaturasra	1_{3x4}	0_{2x4}	1_{3x4}	1_{3x4}	44
	3. Khanda	1_{3x5}	0_{2x5}	1_{3x5}	1_{3x5}	55
	4. Misra	1_{3x7}	0_{2x7}	1_{3x7}	1_{3x7}	77
	5. Sankeerna	1_{3x9}	0_{2x9}	1_{3x9}	1_{3x9}	99
CHATURASRA	1. Tisra	1_{4x3}	0_{2x3}	1_{4x3}	1_{4x3}	42
	2. Chaturasra	1_{4x4}	0_{2x4}	1_{4x4}	1_{4x4}	56
	3. Khanda	1_{4x5}	0_{2x5}	1_{4x5}	1_{4x5}	70
	4. Misra	1_{4x7}	0_{2x7}	1_{4x7}	1_{4x7}	98
	5. Sankeerna	1_{4x9}	0_{2x9}	1_{4x9}	1_{4x9}	126

KHANDA	1.	Tisra	1_{5x3}	0_{2x3}	1_{5x3}	1_{5x3}	51
	2.	Chaturasra	1_{5x4}	0_{2x4}	1_{5x4}	1_{5x4}	68
	3.	Khanda	1_{5x5}	0_{2x5}	1_{5x5}	1_{5x5}	85
	4.	Misra	1_{5x7}	0_{2x7}	1_{5x7}	1_{5x7}	119
	5.	Sankeerna	1_{5x9}	0_{2x9}	1_{5x9}	1_{5x9}	153
MISRA	1.	Tisra	1_{7x3}	0_{2x3}	1_{7x3}	1_{7x3}	69
	2.	Chaturasra	1_{7x4}	0_{2x4}	1_{7x4}	1_{7x4}	92
	3.	Khanda	1_{7x5}	0_{2x5}	1_{7x5}	1_{7x5}	125
	4	Misra	1_{7x7}	0_{2x7}	1_{7x7}	1_{7x7}	161
	5.	Sankeerna	1_{7x9}	0_{2x9}	1_{7x9}	1_{7x9}	207
SANKEERNA	1.	Tisra	1_{9x3}	0_{2x3}	1_{9x3}	1_{9x3}	87
	2.	Chaturasra	1_{9x4}	0_{2x4}	1_{9x4}	1_{9x4}	116
	3.	Khanda	1_{9x5}	0_{2x5}	1_{9x5}	1_{9x5}	145
	4.	Misra	1_{9x7}	0_{2x7}	1_{9x7}	1_{9x7}	203
	5.	Sankeerna	1_{9x9}	0_{2x9}	1_{9x9}	1_{9x9}	261

Similarly, every tala in each of the five varieties *(jaati)* would have five such ramifications, making a total of 35 (5x7) and 175 (35x5) taking all the seven *talas* together.

A composition is thus set to a particular *tala* but it needs to be rendered at a specified speed to bring out its spirit or essence. Three such speeds have been recognised, namely *chowka* (or *vilambita), madhya* and *druta* meaning slow, medium and fast. If a composition is not sung or rendered at the tempo or *laya* which is intended for it, the effect would be lost. The *tala* is, therefore, kept according to the prescribed or intended *laya.*

Kalai is a variant of the *laya* inasmuch as it refers to the tempo or speed of a particular song. A song in any *tala* of double *kalai* is of comparatively slow tempo while single *kalai* songs are racy.

The last attribute *graha* denotes the relationship between the start of the song and that of the *tala.* In other words, it signifies the point of the *tala* at which the song would begin. When the song and the *tala* commence simultaneously, it is called *sama graha.* If the song commences after the *tala* cycle begins, it is known as *anāgata graha* and vice-versa, if the song commences near the end of a *tala* cycle and before the commencement of the next *tala* cycle, it is called *ateeta graha. Graha* is called *eduppu* in Tamil.

Mention should be made here about three techniques that are adopted by a percussionist in Karnatic music and hence, in *Bharata Natyam* also. They are *arudi, mogara* and *mutthaippu*. *Arudi* is a characteristic landing in the middle of a *tala* cycle and generally comes after *teermanam* or *jati*, in *varnam* and *tillana*. *Arudi* is invariably followed by a reposeful pause called *karvai*.

Mogara refers to the percussionist's strokes in series of three generally at the beginning of the song or the dance item.

Mutthaippu is the characteristic finale at the end of a song or stanza.

Mention must be made of some popular *talas* which have not been referred to so far. *Adi tala* and *Chapu tala* are cases in instance. *Adi tala* is kept as one *laghu* with four beats and two *drutas*. It may be easily seen that one *laghu* and two *drutas* represent *triputa tala* and a *laghu* with four beats can therefore be recognised as *chaturasra jaati triputa tala* which is commonly called *Adi tala*. Similarly, what is commonly called as *Chapu tala* is but another way of rendering the *tisra triputa tala*.

DIAGRAMMATIC CHART EXPLAINING *GRAHA*

समोऽतीतोऽनागतश्च ग्रहस्तालो त्रिधा मतः ।

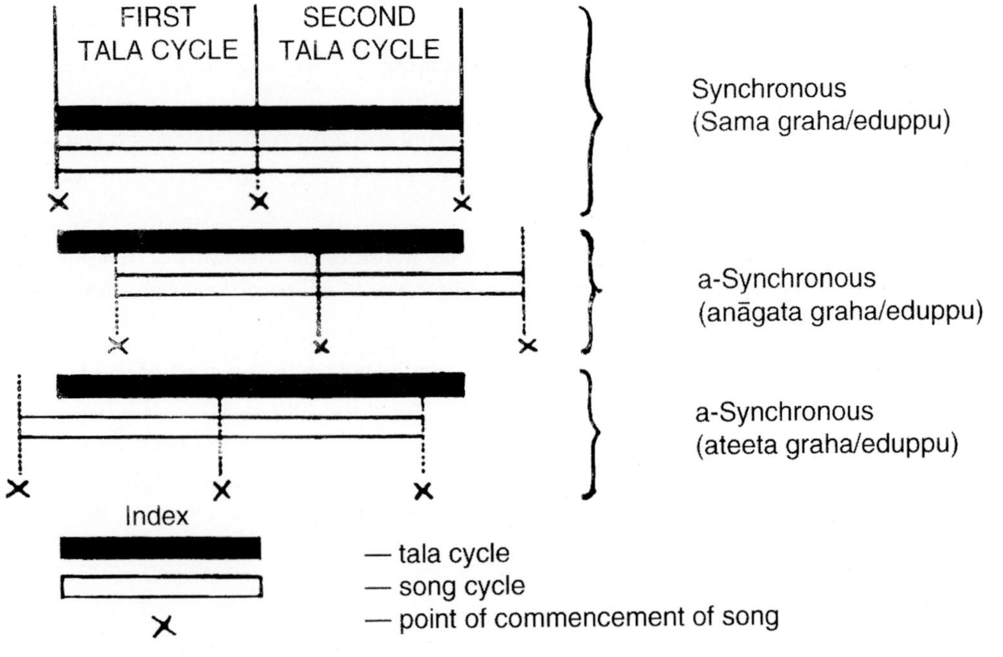

CHAPTER-7

COSTUME AND JEWELLERY

Costume, jewellery and hair style have become so stylised for the different forms of Indian dance that a mere look at the dress and make-up would be enough to identify if it is *Bharata Natyam, Odissi, Kathak, Manipuri, Kathakali* or *Kuchipudi*.

The costume for *Bharata Natyam* is mainly of three styles. Traditionally, a *saree* measuring six yards in length used to be worn such that it could elevate the appearance of the dancer and afford her ease of movement to execute the dance with full occupancy of the stage. However, this manner of tying the saree is somewhat difficult and cumbersome. During the last few decades, therefore, such dress has come to be tailored as a readymade costume and the dress so stitched can be worn easily even as *pyjamas* are worn; and with a blouse in matching or other appropriate colour, it enhances the appearance of the dancer besides affording freedom to move on the stage. A somewhat semi-circular piece to cover the hips, an attachment in front to give a Japanese-fan effect when the dancer bends her legs at the knees and a *melakku* complete the costume. The *melakku* is, however, optional depending on the dancer's wish.

It is also common for dancers to, perform *Bharata Natyam* with a *saree* worn in the style in which it is internationally popular. Here, the saree is stitched in such a way that the ankles are visible and the foot-work is easily seen by the audience. By common custom, this kind of costume is worn while dancing to *padams*, where the emphasis is on expression *(abhinaya)* whereas the traditional style (including the modern tailored version) is, used for regular *nritta* items like *Jatiswaram, Varnam, Tillana* etc.

The list of jewels that adorn a *Bharata Natyam* dancer is long indeed. Starting from the all-too-important ankle-bells, *ghunghroo* in Hindi and *salangai* in Tamil, there are ornaments that are used on various parts of the body from the head to the feet; such as, *Netri Chutti, Surya* and *Chandra, Rākkodi* (jewels worn on the head) the ear rings. *Māttal* (small chains from the ear-ring to the hair on the side of the head) and the *Jimikki* (items that dangle from the ear-rings). These ornaments help heighten the appearance of the artiste. The shining nose-ring *Mookuthi* and the *Bullakku,* a piece fixed to the nostrils, lend lustre. There are the necklaces — long as well as short — as also the bangles on the wrist, *Vangi* around the mid-arm and rings on the fingers. There is the *Ottiyanam* or the ornamental belt around the waist for added effect.

The artiste's hair is decorated with flowers like jasmine, rose or *kanakambaram* and her face is made up for special emphasis through the expression of the eyes. Finally, a red colour liquid is used to beautify the palms, the finger tips and the feet. This colouring material is called *Alta.*

The hair is arranged in a long plait and tied with *kunjalam* made of black colour silken strands. A *jadai* is attached to the plait for embellishment.

COSTUME

FOUR PIECE DRESS

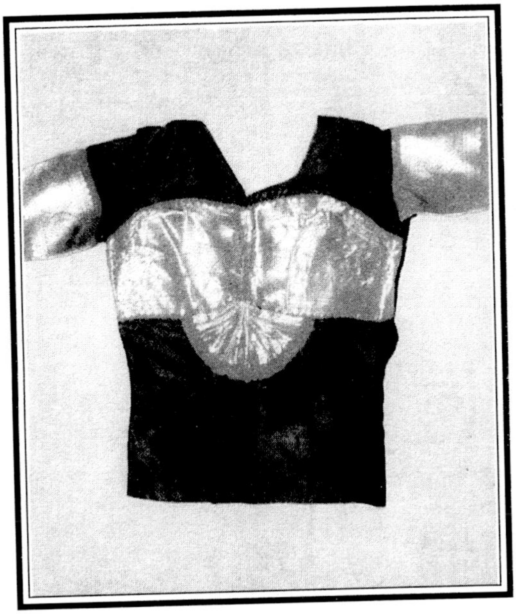

Blouse

Paijama

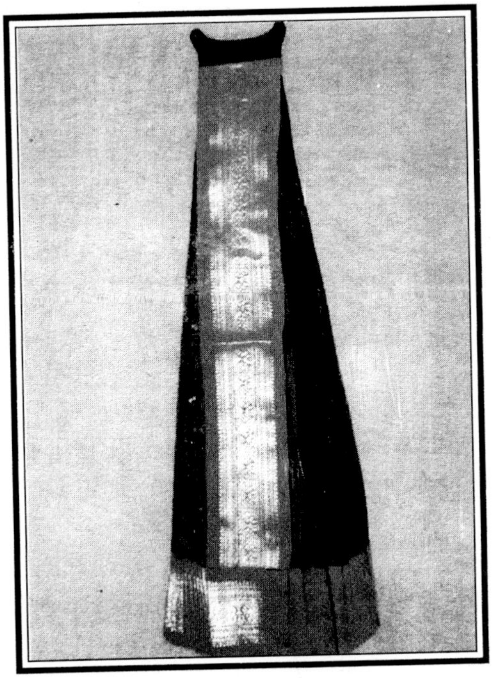

Fan

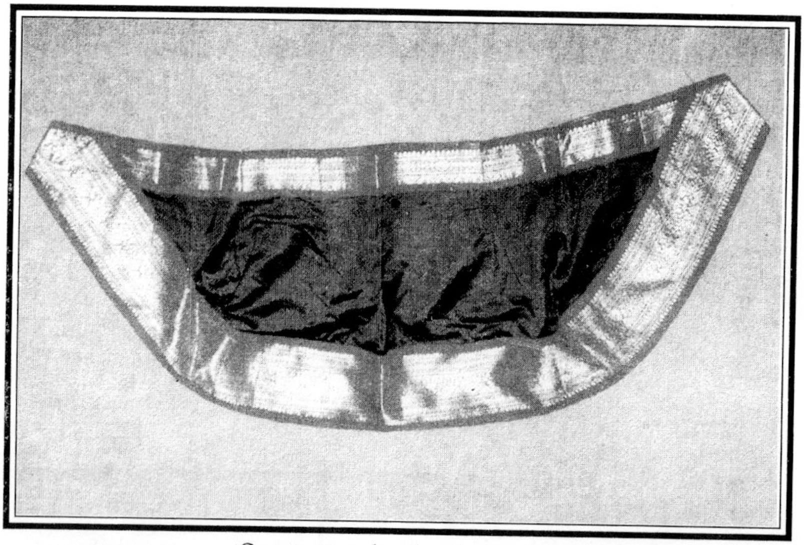

Semi circular back piece

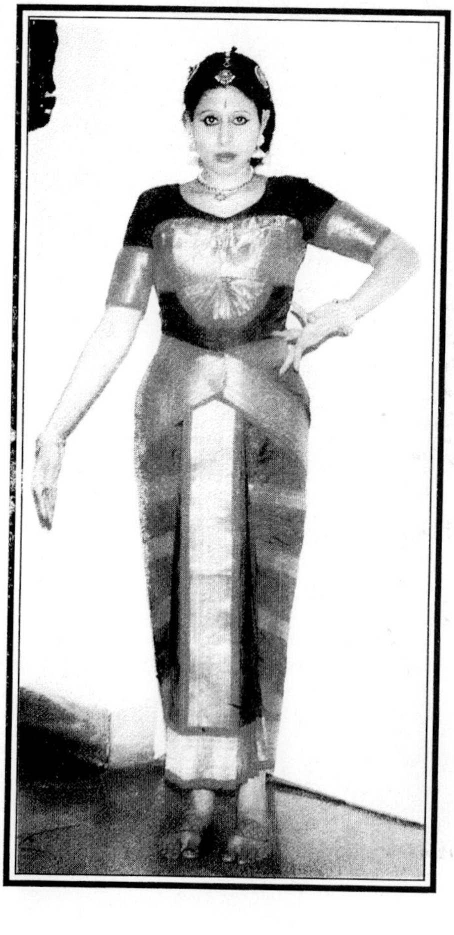

FIVE PIECE DRESS

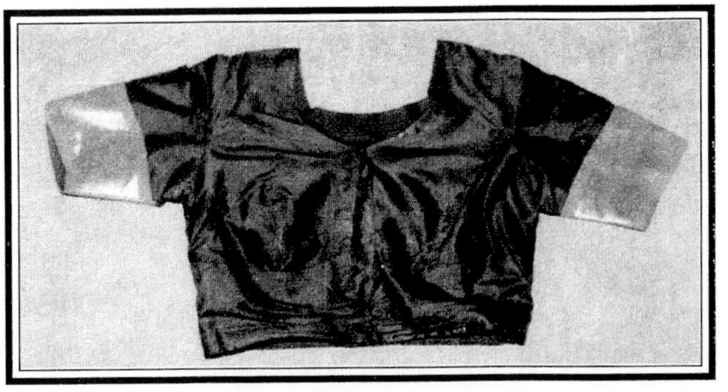

Blouse

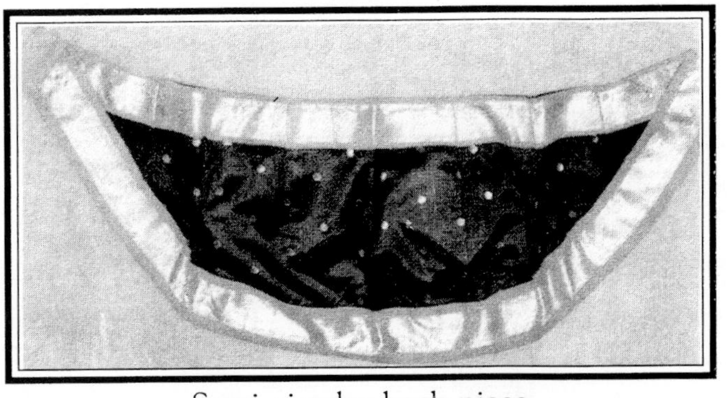

Semi circular back piece

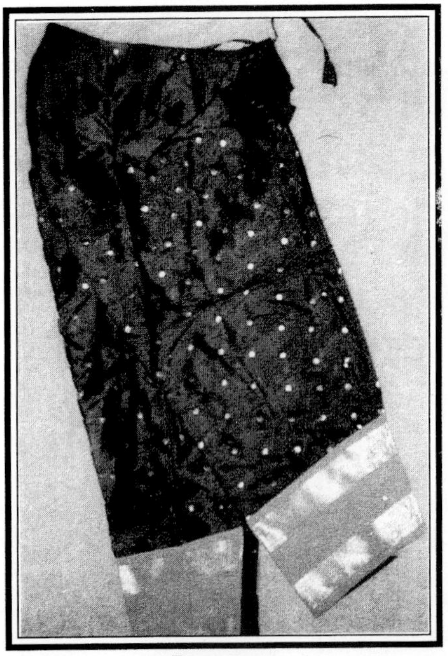

Paijama

Fan

Melakku (Piece over the blouse)

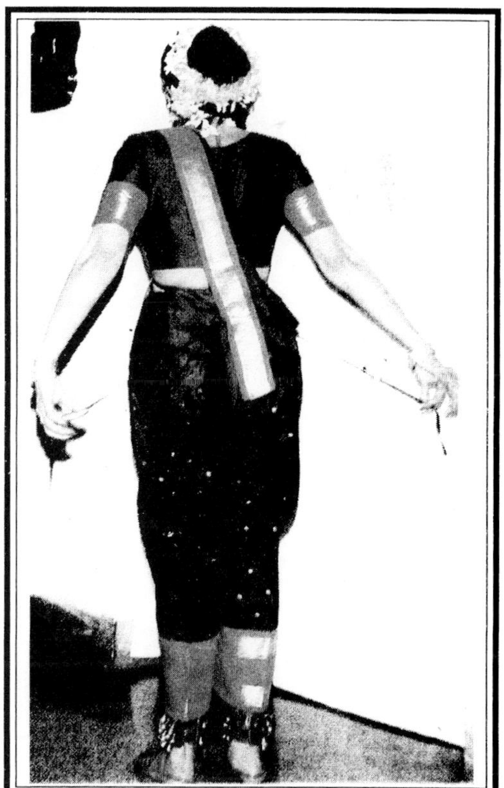

With a short fan

With a long fan

Skirt type dress

Unstitched saree

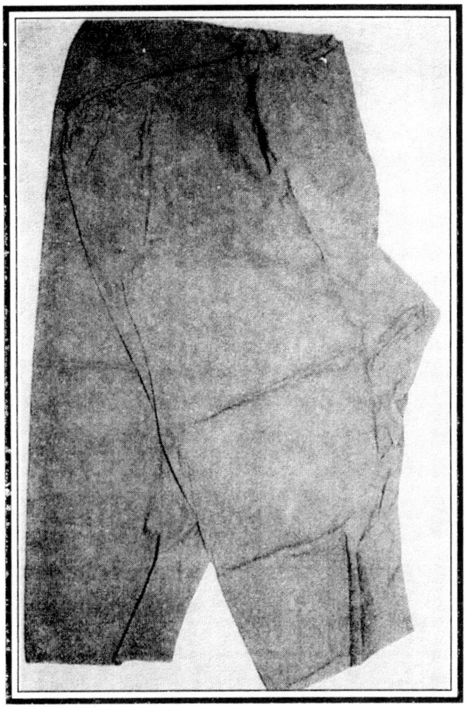

Paijama

Stitched saree with long paijama

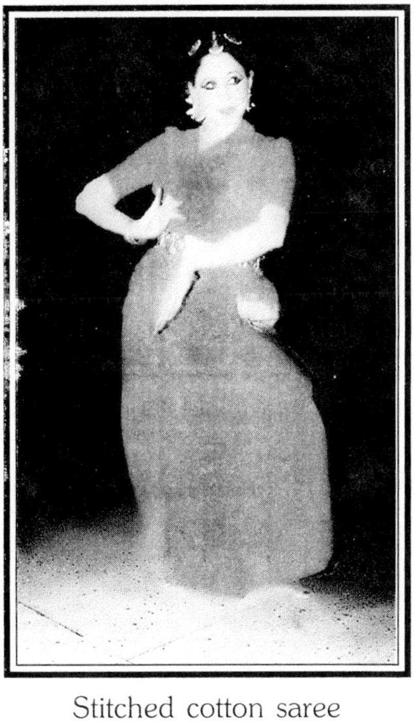

Stitched cotton saree

Dress with long fan without mellakku

JEWELLERY

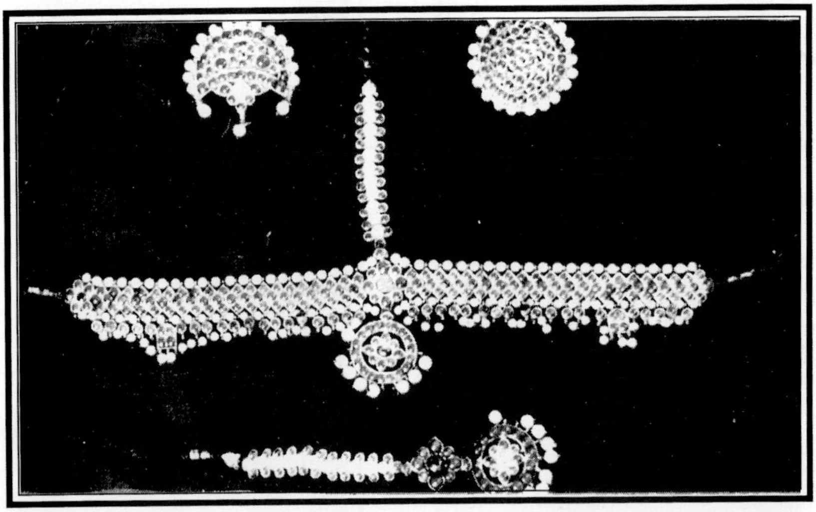

Netri Chutti, Surya-Chandra

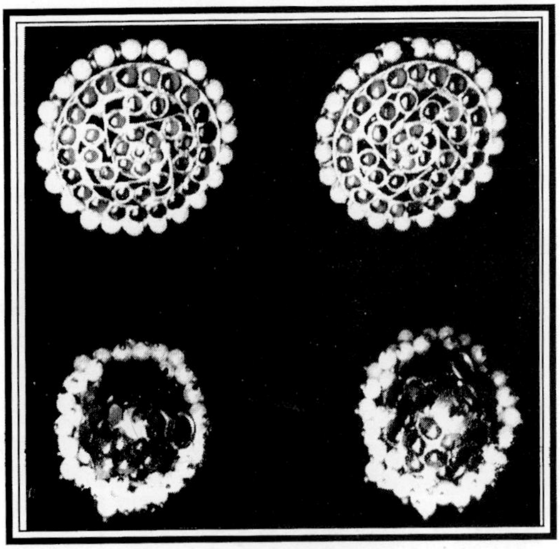

Todu, Jimikki

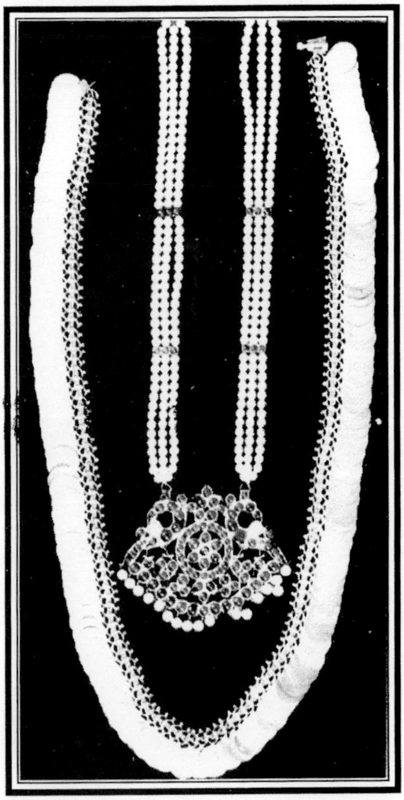

Muthumalai Kasumalai

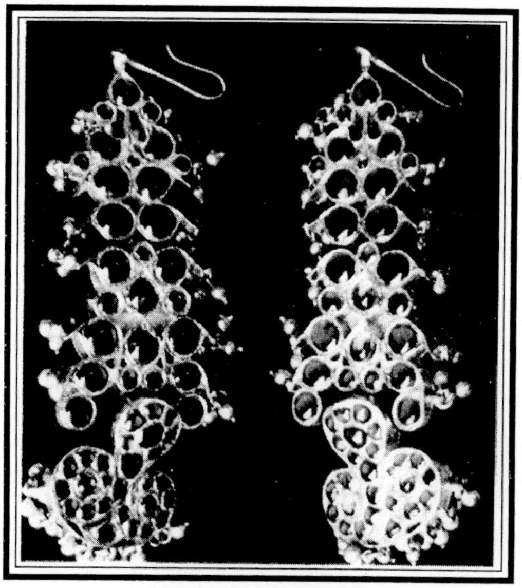

Mattal & Jimmikki

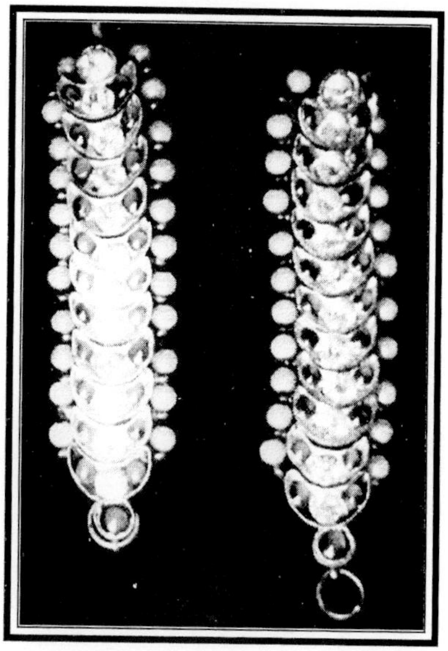

Mattal (another kind)

Mangai Malai & Attikai

Ottiyanam

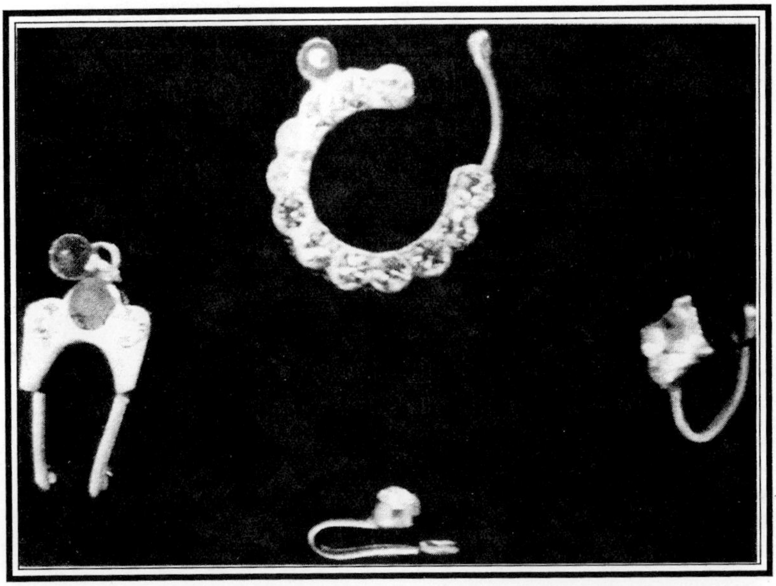

Mukuthi, Nathu, Bullaku

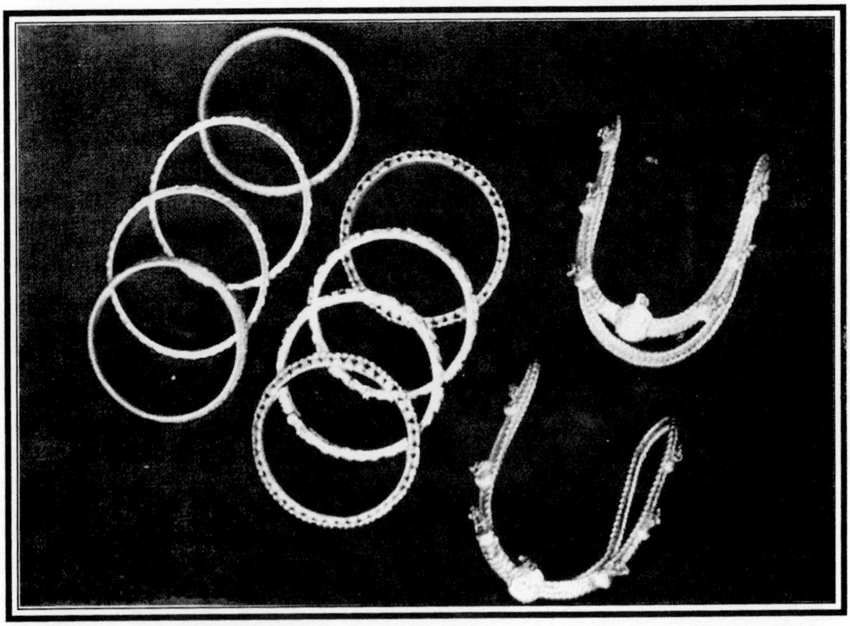

Vangi, Valayal

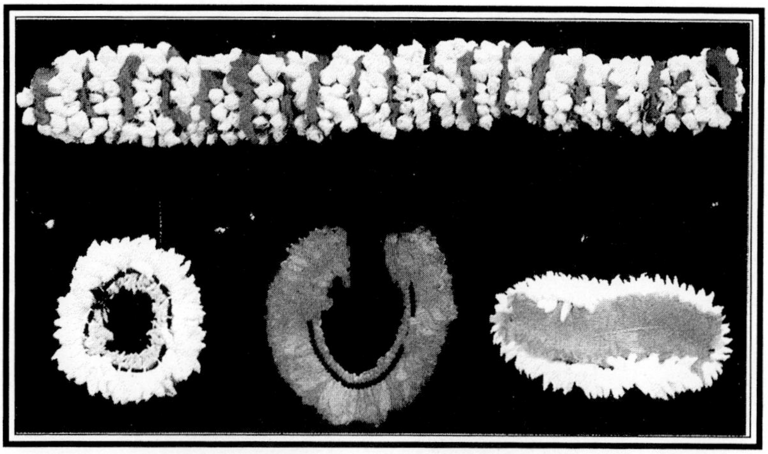

Flowers for the hairs

Kunjalam with thread balls, pearl cups and metal cups

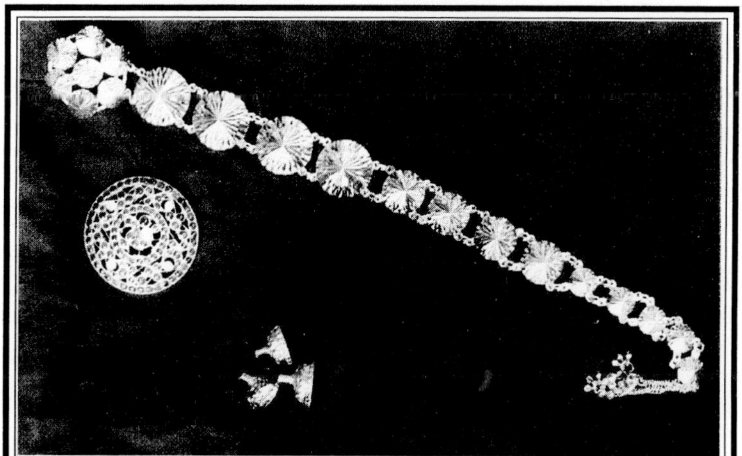

Kunjalam, Rakkoti, Jadai

DIFFERENT TYPES OF HAIR STYLES

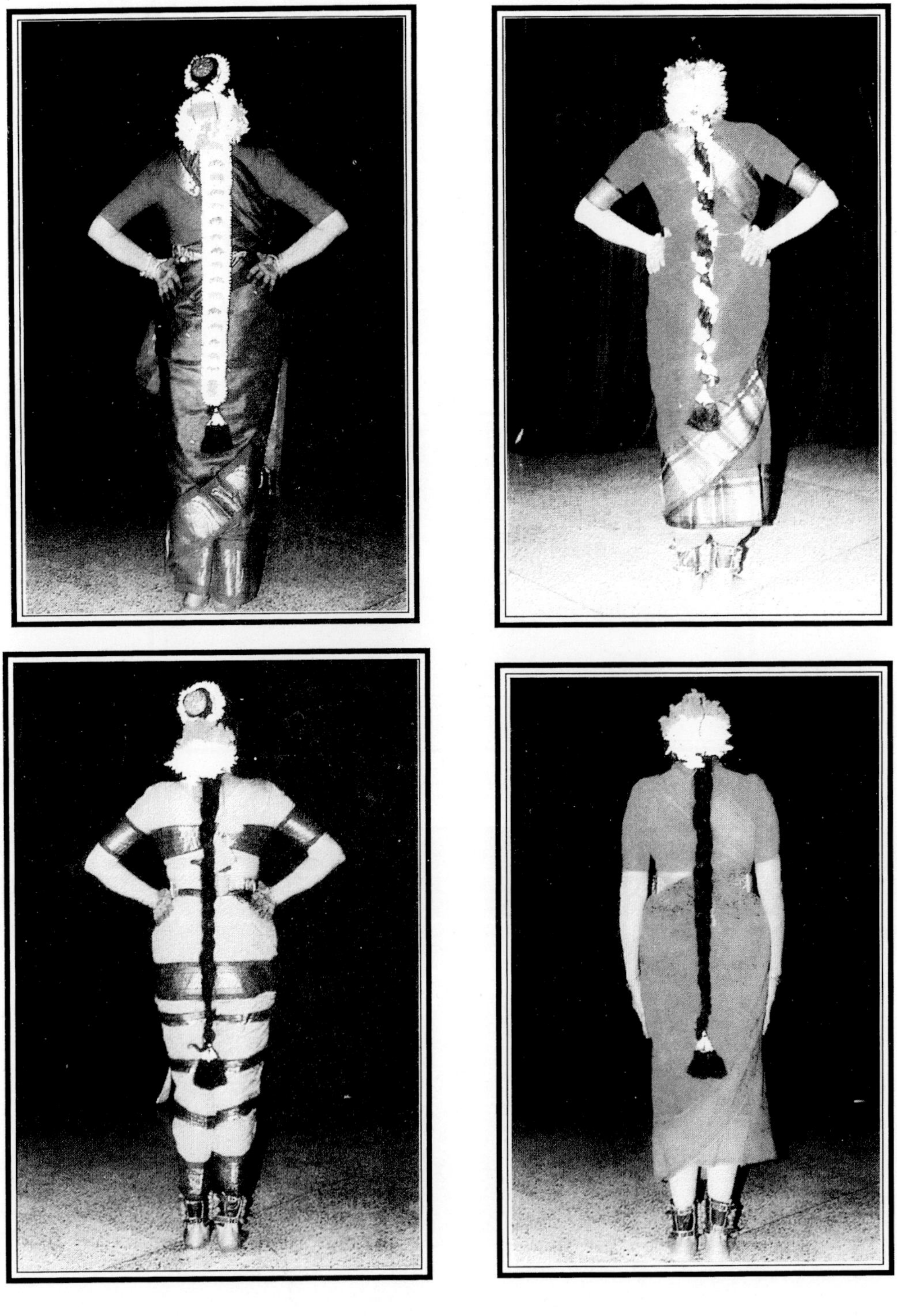

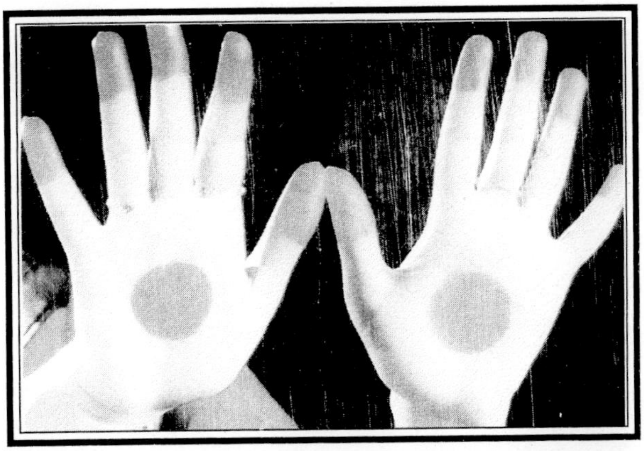

Hands with Alta applied

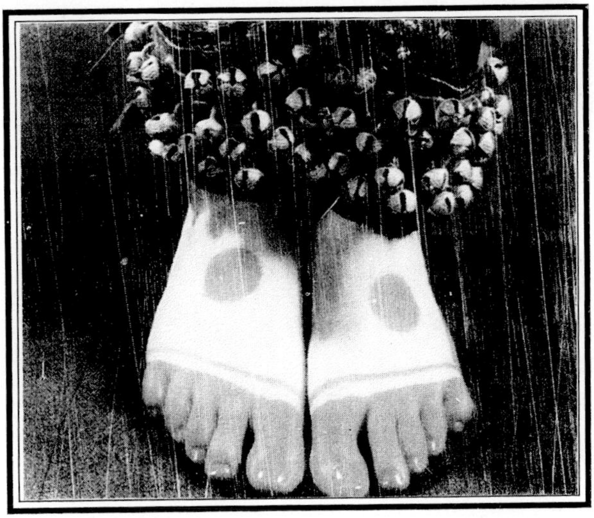

Feet with Alta applied

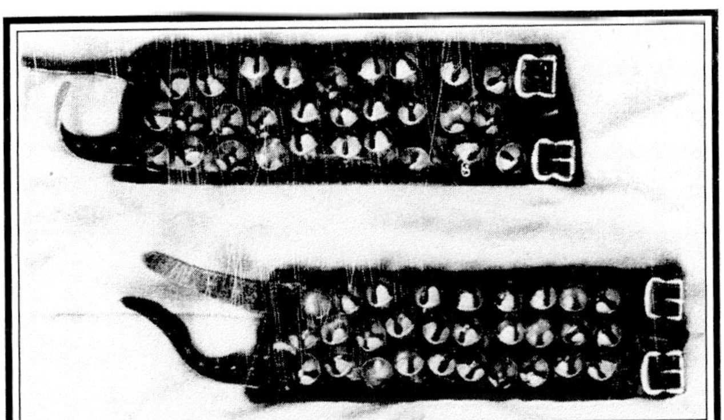

Ghunghroo

Sannidhi Vaidyanathan

CHAPTER-8

MUSICAL INSTRUMENTS

Vocal music is indispensable to *Bharata Natyam* inasmuch as the dominant stress is on *abhinaya* (expression) to bring out the import of a song on the basis of which the particular dance item is choreographed. The vocal singer has to modulate his or her voice to bring out the nuances of the song. In this effort, the singer gets a lot of assistance from the musical instrumentalists who help to produce the optimal effect from the wings. Although violin, harmonium and flute are commonly used as accompaniments to the vocal singer in Karnatic music and hence used for instrumental support in dance recitals also, the instruments that have been traditionally used are the *veena* and the flute, besides the percussion instrument, *mrudangam*. In Sanskrit literature, *veena*, *venu* (flute) and *mrudangam* are described as the musical instruments of the *Devas*.

Veena and violin fall under the category of stringed instruments while the flute and the harmonium are classified as wind instruments. *Shruti* or pitch is maintained by the *tanpura*, a stringed instrument or a *shruti-box*, a wind instrument. Now-a-days an electronic instrument is also used to provide the pitch for the singer. The percussionist plays the *jatis*, *korvais* and *teermanams* on the *mrudangam* besides accompanying the vocal singer. A passing mention may be made of two other percussion instruments namely, *kanjeera* and *ghatam* which can be played to produce sounds to conform to the *jati*, *korvai* and *teermanam*. Although not often seen in *Bharata Natyam* recitals of late, these two instruments could also very well be part of the musical set-up. A point to remember is, however, that while *mrudangam* is a necessary and sufficient percussion support for any recital, dance as well as music, neither *kanjeera* nor *ghatam* can be the lone percussion instrument for a programme, they can only be an adjunct to *mrudangam,* which is the mainstay.

That brings us to the cymbals with which the *Guru* or the *Nattuvanar* (conductor) guides and controls the dancer's foot-work as well as the vocal singer and the orchestra. The cymbals are called *talam,* possibly on account of the sounds that the metallic pieces give out when struck against each other. The *Nattuvanar,* by skilful handling of the cymbals, produces sounds resembling the *jatis, korvais* and *teermanams* so that they form the cue for the dancer, the singer and the orchestra alike. In a dance recital, the *Nattuvanar* utters, now and then, the *Soilukattu,* a Tamil word to indicate the rhythmic syllables denoting the *jati* and *teermanam,* to add the master's touch to it.

The traditional instruments are often referred to in the songs which are selected for the *Bharata Natyam* since these instruments are associated with one or the other of the Gods in the pantheon of the Hindu mythology. For instance, flute is Lord *Krishna's* favourite instrument with which he produced such divine notes sending the *gopis* into raptures. So too is *veena* associated with *Saraswati,* the Goddess of Learning, seated on a white lotus. *Nandi* is said to have accompanied on the *mrudangam,* when Lord *Shiva* performed the cosmic *tandava* dance. The *tandava* dance had other accompaniments too— Lord *Brahma* wielding the cymbals and *Narada Muni* with the *tanpura* providing vocal music.

TĀLAM

STRING INSTRUMENTS

VIOLIN

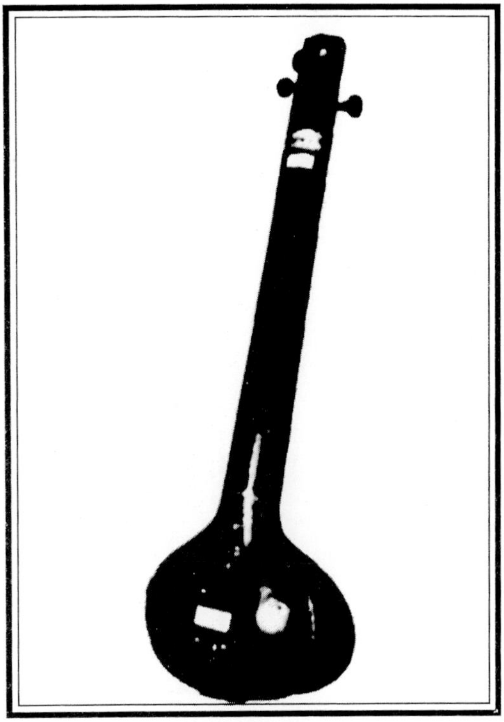

TANPURA

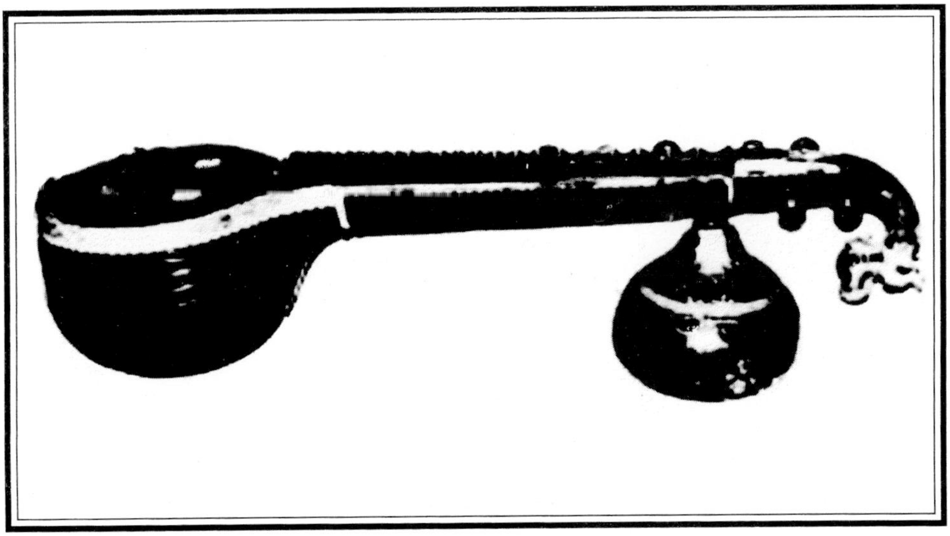

VEENA

WIND INSTRUMENTS

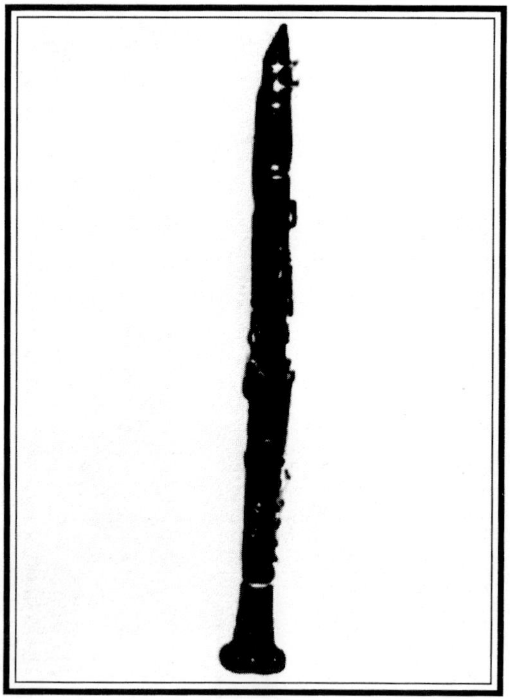

CLARIONET

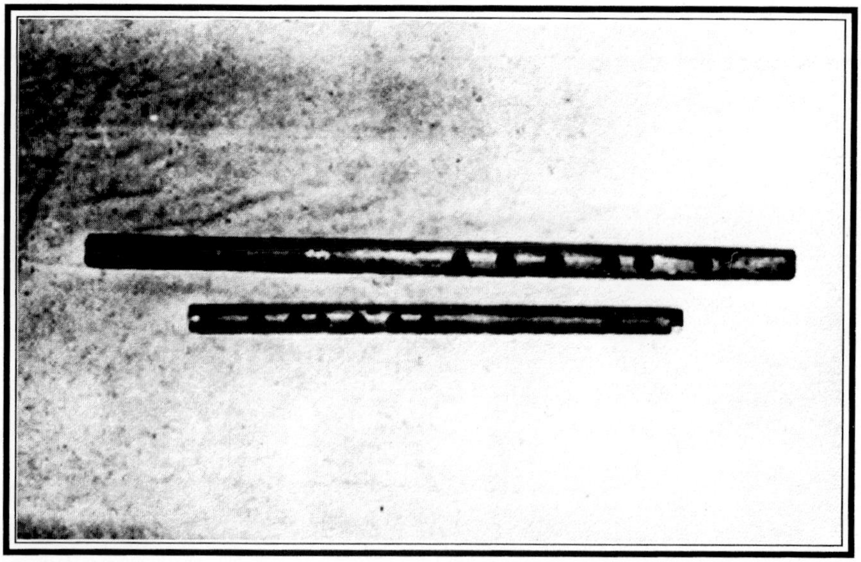

FLUTE

HARMONIUM

SHRUTI BOX

PERCUSSION INSTRUMENTS

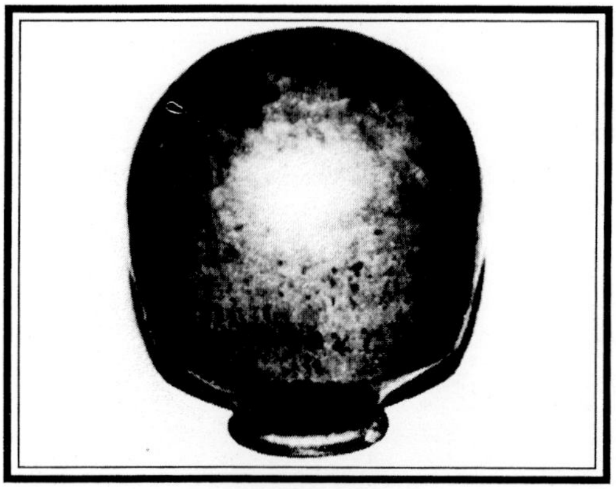

GHATAM

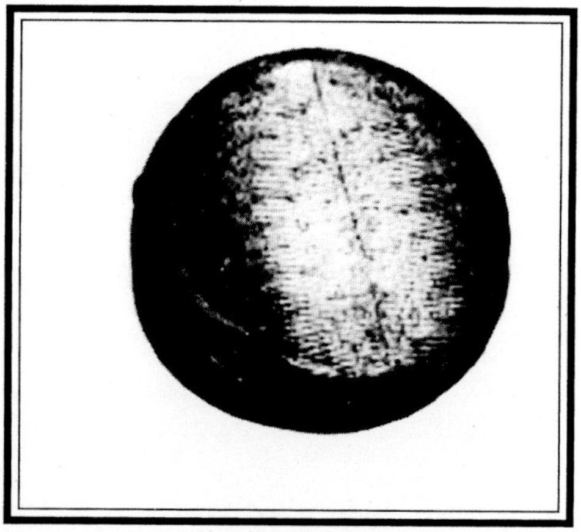

KANJEERA

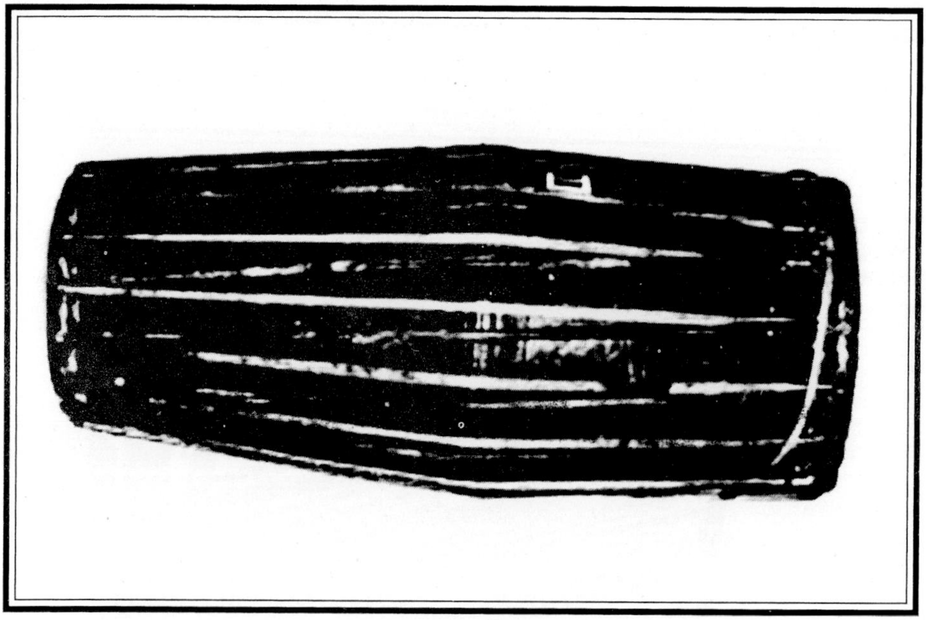

MRUDANGAM

CHAPTER-9

ARANGETRAM
(Maiden Performance)

GURU

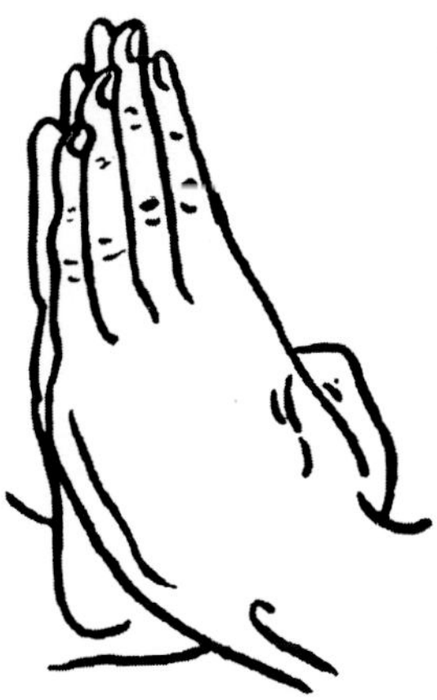

SHISHYA

This ancient art of *Bharata Natyam* has been handed down from generation to generation through the *guru-shishya parampara* or the master-disciple tradition. It is at a fairly tender age that the student is initiated in the art on an auspicious day. Yes, it should be a tender age but not too tender. Preferably, the training should start after the aspiring student attains the age of seven years. Any performing artiste, particularly a dancer, needs a good, well-built personality. Experience has shown that if the training is commenced before the age of seven years, the growth of the child is inhibited, making it difficult for her to be presentable to the audience.

There are some shlokas depicting the essential characteristics, qualifications and disqualifications of a danseuse in *Nandikeswara's Abhinayatarpana.*

पात्रलक्षणम्

तनूवी रूपवती श्यामा पीनोन्नपतयोधरा
प्रगल्भा सरसा कान्ता कुशला ग्रहमोक्षयोः।
विशाललोचना गीतवाद्यतालानुवर्तिनी
पराध्र्यभूषासम्पन्ना प्रसन्नमुखपङ्कजा।
एवंविधगुणोपेता नर्तकी समुदीरिता।।

Slim bodied, young, having large eyes and well developed breasts, jovial, co-ordinating well with the accompaniments in music and beats, knowing when to start and end the rectial, having colourful dresses and beautiful are the characteristics of a danseuse.

वर्जनीयपात्राणि
पुष्पाक्षी केशहीना च स्थूलोष्ठी लम्बितस्तनी।
अतिस्थूलाप्यतिकृशा अत्युच्चाप्यतिवामना।।
कुब्जा च स्वरहीना च दशैता नाट्यवर्जिताः।

पात्रस्य प्राणा
जवः स्थिरत्वं रेखा च भ्रमरी दृषिटरश्रमः।।
मेघा श्रद्धा वचो गीतं पात्रप्राणा दश स्मृताः।
एवंविधेन पात्रेण नृत्यं कार्यं विधानतः।।

Disqualifications: Thick lips, undeveloped breasts, very fat or lean, very tall or very short, scanty hair, hunchback, lack of abilities at music.

Essentials: Devotion, good knowledge of music and singing, clear speech, memory and devotion, stability, endurance and attractive look.

BETEL LEAF, BETEL NUT, AGARBATI, FRUITS, CAMPHOR, COCOANUT, KUM-KUM, SANDALWOOD PASTE

The initiation is almost a ceremony with the parents taking the child to the *guru* who is offered cocoanut, betel leaves, supari, fruits, and flowers. The formal training commences with the girl paying obeisance to the *guru*. The obeisance is offered by the student in the standing posture with the heels together and the hands (bent inwards at the wrist) on the waist. Thereafter with the *shikhara hasta,* she brings both the hands to the front in a circular motion, beats two steps and bends to touch the floor with the hands now in *dolā hasta.* She then gets up with the hands in the *anjali hasta* and regains the original standing position with the heels together and the hands on the waist. The *guru* also teaches her to adopt the *ardha mandala* posture, with the heels together and legs bent at the knee. This is a classical posture of *Bharata Natyam* and is assumed several times in the course of a recital. The *guru* uses the *tattu kazhi* and the *talam* (see illustrations) for conducting the classes and the performance respectively.

TĀLAM AND TATTU KAZHI

The syllabus of a course in *Bharata Natyam* is so drawn up that it enables the students to pick up, step by step, the intricacies of the art. It is methodical, systematic and scientific. Starting with a vigorous training in foot-work with the *ardha mandala* posture, the student is taken through a course of movements of the hands, the neck and the eyes to represent various feelings and expressions and to provide specific effects. Since the foot-work consists of a series of *Adavu* (called *Korvai, Jati* and *Teermanam)* in the different beats, this grounding is a must before the regular items of dance are learnt.

Practice is of utmost importance since that is what brings perfection to the artiste and her recital. After a good deal of practice in the basics, the student becomes ripe for learning the regular items, which can be classified under six categories namely:

Alārippu

Jatiswaram

Sabdam

Varnam

Tillāna

Padam

ALĀRIPPU (Nritta)

This is the first course in the entire syllabus, that the *shishya* is taught, after a rigorous training in *Hasta, Bheda, Adavus* and *Abhinaya.* This course essentially invokes the blessings of God, the Guru and the audience and hence is always the first to be performed. Its usefulness lies in helping to loosen the limbs and preparing the artiste for the subsequent items. This is a piece involving rhythmic and enchanting movements of the eyes, the neck and the hands.

In the standing and the *ardhamandala* postures, elementary *adavus* are executed. Only the *sollukuttu*—rhythmic phrases—is rendered by the *Guru* with no song being sung. Generally this course is taught in *tisra (3), chaturasra (4), khanda (5), misra (7)* and *sankeerna (9)* beats.

JATISWARAM (Nritta)

This section of the syllabus deals with the execution of adavus and mudras. combined in definite groups. Thus, the student learns to perform simple *korvais* and *jatis.* This course being *swara-cum-jati,* the *jatis* are executed a number of times with the support of musical notes *(swara).* Mostly the accompanying music has no meaning since the main emphasis here is on coordination of adavus. Nritta hastas are used in this course. Generally, this number is done in *Rupaka tala* having six matras.

SABDAM (Nritya)

This introduces the student to another important aspect of dance — *abhinaya.* This course focusses mainly on the face and the facial expressions. The student is taught to express the *navabhava* through *bhedas* and *hastas.*

The song is generally based on a mythological theme, giving ample opportunities to the student to portray the characters and emotions with the help of *bhedas, mudras* and *navabhava.*

This number is normally performed in *chapu-tala* (seven beats): Ta-ki-ta-ta-ka-dhi-mi.

VARNAM (Nritta & Nritya)

This course constitutes, more or less a challenge to the *shishya.* The *varnam* requires the rendering of *korvais, jatis* and *teermanams* on the one hand and the *abhinaya* on the other, alternately. The student is trained to display her abilities in a comprehensive manner. The *guru* utters the rhythmic syllables *(Sollukattu* in Tamil and *bol* in Hindi) particularly for the *teermanams* in a *varnam.* The essential *bhava* in a *varnam* is *rati (Sringara rasa).*

TILLANA (Nritta)

The emphasis in this course is once again on footwork. It is a vigorous number requiring exquisite execution of intricate steps *(korvais)* in three speeds and five *gatis* (3, 4, 5, 7 & 9). Generally, tillana is sung in adi tal. Mostly, *nritta hastas* are used in this course.

Being a fast rhythmic piece working upto a crescends of speed with elegance, it provides a substantial scope to the student to perfect her footwork.

PADAM (Nritya)

In this last course, the student is initiated into the finer nuances of *abhinaya.* This is different from *sabdam* in the sense that while the latter involves elementary or basic expressions of emotions, *padam* goes into much more elaborate and intricate expression of the *bhavas,* through *bhedas, hastas* and *adavus.*

These padams are normally in verse from and hence lend themselves to choreography to bring out their essence. Therefore they provide ideal situations for the student to display skill with much finesse and refinement, as befits the character portrayed.

Once the student has learnt these items, she is ready for the *arangetram.* This again is a Tamil word consisting of two parts, '*arangu*' meaning the stage and '*etram*' meaning ascending. In other words, the *arangetram* signifies the artiste's maiden public performance. It marks the culmination of the first phase of the dancer's career and she may be said to graduate to the stage of being able to give regular solo performances. The *arangetram* is done in the presence of a distinguished and elite audience and knowledgeable critics to prove beyond doubt the artiste's ability as a solo performer of the art. The *arangetram* is conducted by the *guru* and on the successful completion of the *arangetram,* the *guru* is honoured with flowers, fruits and the conventional *guru-dakshina* by the disciple and her parents. In a sense, *arangetram* can be compared with the graduation of a University student but it differs from the latter in a vital respect. On completion of the University course, the student usually parts company with the teacher(s) but in *Bharata Natyam,* the master-disciple nexus continues even after the disciple starts giving public recitals regularly. It represents a system of continuing education to enable the disciple to imbibe fully the intricacies and the technique of the art so that in due time, she can acquire poise and confidence and with maturity, blossom into a consummate dancer. *Bharata Natyam* is a perfect model of synchronisation of many arts and aspects of beauty. It is a combination of *Nritta* and *Nritya,* religious devotion, philosophy and cosmic truth. Hence, there is no short cut even for a genius to become proficient in the art. It requires years of proper and patient training under masters of authentic traditions and proper development and utilisation of one's own intelligence and imagination.

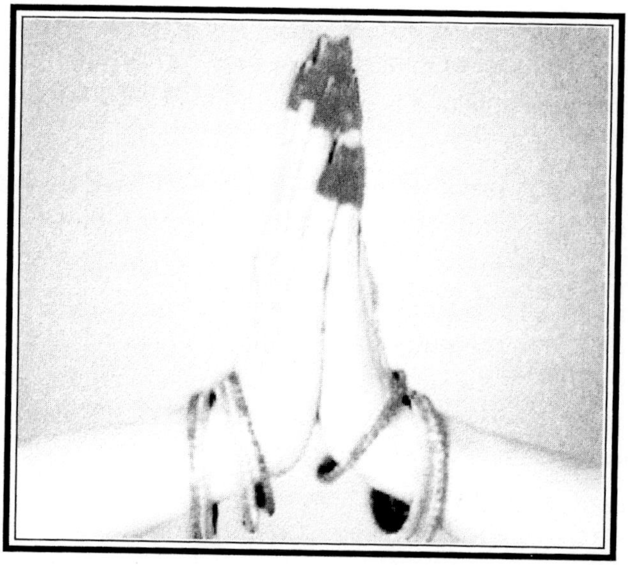

DIAGRAMMATIC REPRESENTATION OF THE ELEMENTS OF BHARATA NATYAM

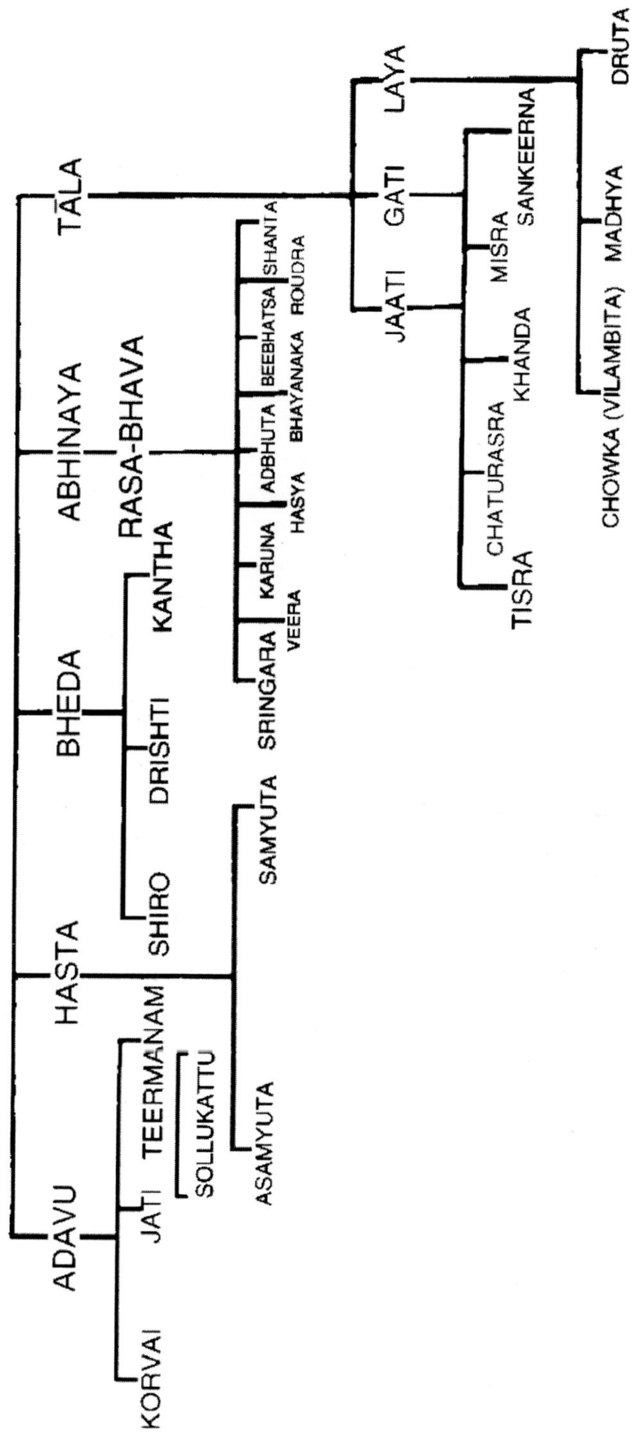

ASCENDING STEPS OF THE SYLLABUS OF BHARATA NATYAM

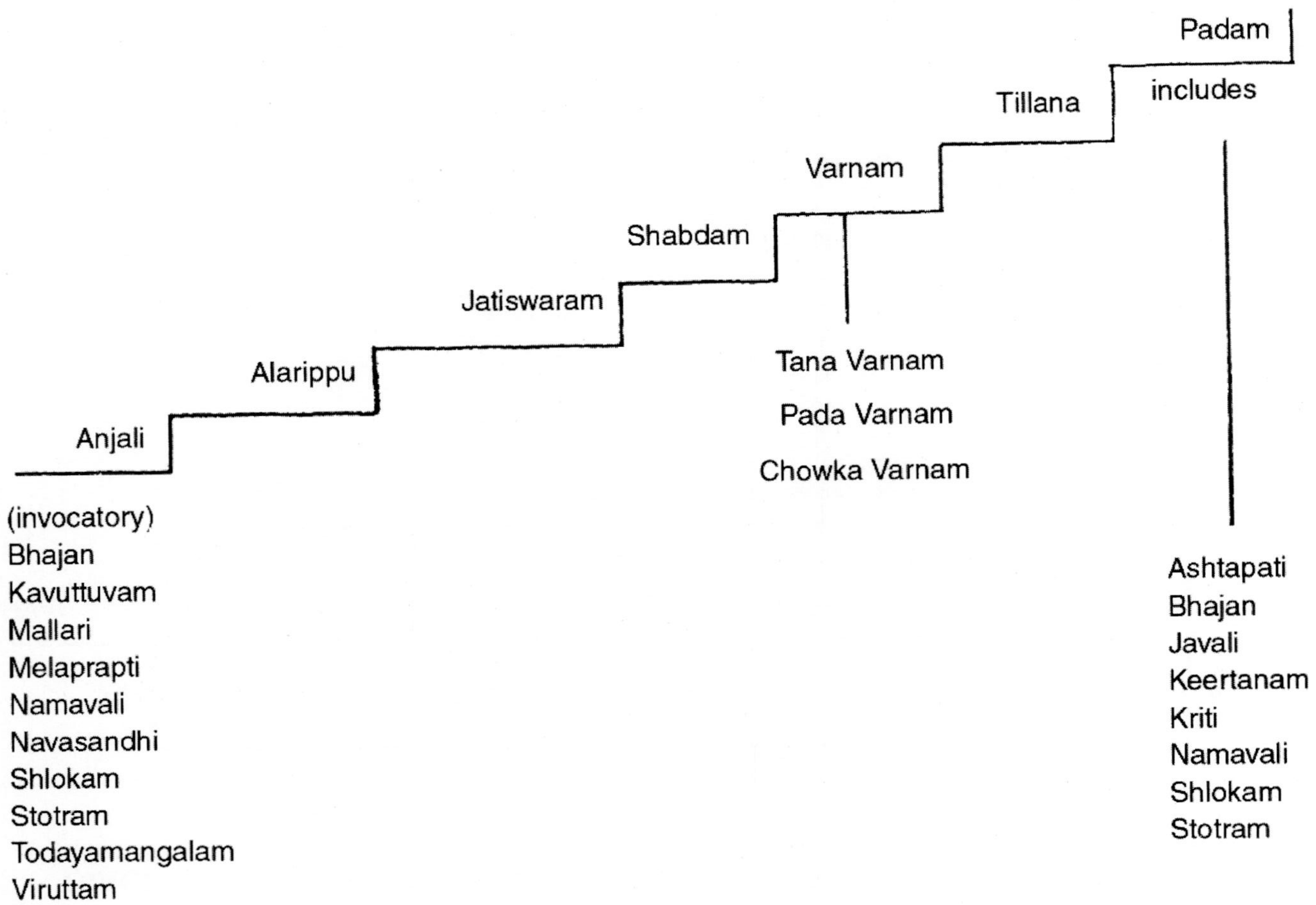

INDEX

A

B

C

D

E

F

G

H

I

J

K

S

T

U

V

W

Y

Z